Beyond
Beyond

Beyond
Beyond

A CHANCE ENCOUNTER,
AN ONLINE COURTSHIP &
THE LANGUAGE OF LOVE

Roz Lewy & Ralph Insinger
Illustrations by Ralph Insinger

SUSAN SCHADT PRESS

AN "INTRODUCTION"
IS IN ORDER …

Dear Reader,

We are faced with a dilemma. How do we write an introduction to experiences and developments that could not be anticipated or planned?

When the unlikely outcome seems incredulous in reflection, we have decided to just invite you to meet US and join US on our very special journey ... one you might take in your lifetime!

Since we will be reading together informally, on a first name basis, let us introduce ourselves ... Roz (a widow of years and Karen's and Steve's Mom) and Ralph (a recent widower and Mori's Dad).

Join us with a turn of the page.

R&R

From: Karen
Sent: Wednesday, August 15, 2018 at 6:41 AM
To: Roz
Subject: Fwd: Sweet dreams

FYI ... :)

Sent from my iPhone

Begin forwarded message:
From: RALPH
Date: Tuesday, August 14, 2018 at 11:40 PM
To: Karen
Subject: Sweet dreams

Hello Karen,
It has gotten late and in all likelihood you and your mother have already entered dreamland. You must have had a busy day, trying to make every moment special as you use the time remaining for her here. You've earned some rest.

Bedtime beckons me too, but I wanted to take a moment to recap my day and want you to know how memorable it was. Your suggestion to dine at the Museum of Fine Arts was such a good idea and having your mother with us really enhanced the conversation. And how often does one savor great art as a prelude to dining? Thank you for providing your guest pass to get me into the museum. I was supposed to be taking you to lunch, but you made it happen.

Extend my best wishes to Rosalind for a safe and comfortable trip back to her home. It would be a "pleasure" to see her again, perhaps on a future trip to Boston.

I'm closing the day smiling!
Ralph

From: Roz
Sent: Wednesday, August 15, 2018 at 11:33 AM
To: RALPH
Subject: Thank You!

Ralph,
Thank you for lunch. It was nice meeting you yesterday and realizing the extraordinary coincidences of life chapters that kept surprisingly occurring during our lunch conversation.

I am so delighted to know of your relationship with Karen and to know how much she admires you and to observe your appreciation of her. I am very proud of Karen's professional success and more importantly, the woman she is.

I envy your nostalgic road trip and am guessing memories will abound. Taking time to visit meaningful places and reconnecting with important people in your life is always personally satisfying and fulfilling.

Travel well and enjoy the moments!
Roz

Sent from my iPhone

From: RALPH
Sent: Wednesday, August 15, 2018 at 2:15 PM
To: Roz
Subject: Re: Thank You!

Hi Roz,
It was such a nice message you sent. You're welcome for the lunch, but no need to thank me ... I had all the pleasure. I'm sorry your soup wasn't so great. We'll try again when you're back in Boston.

You are so right about the coincidences that show up in our lives. Hearing of your Missouri roots immediately made me feel more acquainted with you.

Your pride in Karen is borne out, considering her qualifications and accomplishments. She covers a lot of ground and has an amazing awareness of all of it. Her spirit elevates mine every time I am with her.

I appreciated your comments about my upcoming travel, and agree, staying in touch with the important people in our lives is too vital to let lapse. Being "single" again has certainly clarified that.

I know you must have had a wonderful time with Karen, and your grandkids too. Safe travel now as you go home. My personal hope is to get to see you again.

Ralph

• • •

From: Roz
Sent: Sunday, August 26, 2018 at 2:09 PM
To: RALPH
Subject: Happy Sunday!

Ralph,
Hope you are enjoying your weekend. Funny how things happen ... my granddaughter is experiencing Freshman Orientation at Webster University these last few days and although the campus is some miles from St Louis proper, I found myself thinking about our lunch at the MFA and the Missouri connection. I am guessing you are finalizing your plans for your sojourn West in early September.

Listening to my son (there settling his daughter into the dorm) commenting on the beauty and "wholesomeness" of this Midwest college town gave me a twinge of nostalgia ... curious how roots remain despite the passage of time.

Now that I am home again in "the land of the swaying palms" with "re-entry"behind me ... the penalty one pays for being away for an extended time, I miss Karen and family and look forward to our next togetherness ... perhaps for Thanksgiving.

Take care and travel safely.
Roz

Sent from my iPhone

From: RALPH
Sent: Sunday, August 26, 2018 at 9:57 PM
To: Roz
Subject: Re: Happy Sunday!

Hello Roz,
Finding your message in my inbox was the highlight of my day. How sweet it was!

The weekend here has been very pleasant. Yesterday the temperature moderated, and I was outdoors in sunshine, about 73 degrees. It was perfect. Today it got up into the low 80's but breezy and nice.

I've thought back to the lunch we spent together, and it was delightful to chat with you. Of course, with Karen as well. After you arrived back home, did you wish you would have spent a few more days in Boston?

When I completed my military service in Germany and was preparing to ship out for home, I thought maybe I should take my discharge abroad, and live and work there for a while. But I thought my family and friends were too important, so I went back to Missouri. Within a couple weeks I was asking myself, "What were you thinking?"

Your point about how one's "roots"remain despite the passage of time rings true with me. While I wouldn't want to move back to St. Charles where I was born and grew up, I do have the attraction to return occasionally to connect with a few friends I always admired, who have remained in the town all their lives. However, I'm turned off about the locale due to what has been done physically to the townscape/ landscape, the poor judgment that permitted devastating such a significantly historic town with shoddy new development.

My plans are settled for traveling shortly after Labor Day. I've confirmed the dates of my stopovers, everyone excited about picking up from where we last left off. I think I'm going to enjoy the freedom of the open road.

I'm glad you're comfortable getting away from home every so often. There's a sense of adventure in that. My parents were of an earlier generation that always felt secure being back in their nest. When my mom and dad visited with us, after four or five days my mom would say, "Well, dad, I guess we should plan to return home tomorrow or the next day."

We would ask her what was so important, and she would tell us, "Well, the grass will need cutting!" Isn't that a hoot?

So I'm impressed that you're already planning for your next visit. I hope you and Karen will have such a loose schedule that there will be room to fit me in. Roz, I'd love to visit with you more. You take care too and thank you for your good wishes.

Ralph

• • •

From: Roz
Sent: Friday, August 31, 2018 at 9:31 AM
To: RALPH
Subject: "The Open Road"

I am smiling reading your email, Ralph. If you would like company along the long stretches of "the open road" here is my phone number ... actually, if you want to chat, call me anytime!

Roz

Sent from my iPhone

From: RALPH
Sent: Friday, August 31, 2018 at 12:32 PM
To: Roz
Subject: Re: "The Open Road"

Hi Roz,
What a generous offer, to give me your phone number for relief, those times when the road begins to mesmerize me, or if I observe something extraordinary that I want to share. Finding your email this morning made me realize I never acknowledged your previous similar email. I'm sorry about that.

This week I've been fraught with so many simple things to get done before I depart for almost three weeks. Just the accounting is unusual ... ! Normally I am down to the wire paying my bills. Now I'm paying weeks ahead of the due dates. I'm finally getting around to some household chores too, so the place is in order when I get home again.

August 29, 2018

Dear Roz,

We're suffering 93° today, which is one reason I'm indoors writing to you. I hope things are milder by you.

While cleaning up around here I came upon some magazines that my wife had saved. One was "YANKEE", all about New England, which my wife enjoyed. As I browsed into it I found a couple interesting items and thought you might like to see them too.

The one about pottery presents a distinctive technique for decorating the ceramic ware and the potters graphics related to ocean life are beautifully done, in color and composition.

The other piece with photos of the last of the hill farms appealed to me because it presents landscapes and farm folk who are so much like the environment in which I grew up. It brought back so many satisfying memories of my boyhood.

You may keep these or pass them along to others. Perhaps you have some similar nostalgic memories..

Regards, Ralph

You can expect to hear from me. Meanwhile take care. BTW here is my cell number.

Hope you have a great holiday.
Ralph

From: Roz
Sent: Saturday, September 1, 2018 at 2:42 PM
To: RALPH
Subject: Your Posted Articles

Dear Ralph,
Surprise for Me! I just picked up today's mail and found your large white envelope (very formally addressed) sharing articles. Coincidentally, during the 19 years we had a home on Lake Winnipesaukee (Moultonborough, NH), I often read "Yankee" and enjoyed learning about local artisans, happenings in the area, the best fresh produce to purchase, and where the farm stands could be found.

The article about potters is fun to read since I became friendly with a local potter in Wolfeboro, NH during our years on Lake Winni (a 40 minute drive around the lake or 20 minute ride by boat). The shop was on the Main Street and was a necessary stop (many of the pieces are visible and used in my house) on every outing to Wolfeboro. The potter's decorative pottery is charming and useful ... many of my friends over the years would make purchases from the shop during their visits with us. Love these coincidences!

Needless to say, it is nice to see pictures that can resonate in a personal way with memories of meaning for us. Rural life has many riches beyond the soil.

Can't help commenting on your beautiful penmanship. As a former high school English teacher ... one who read more essays in long hand (before the computer destroyed the art of the pen) than one can count, I could not help but be aware of and appreciative of readable penmanship. Over the years, I would find myself wondering about how in many instances, the essay penmanship reflected a bit of the personality of the student, the size and clarity of letters, the visual appearance of the scroll and the slant of the words. Let me know if you are curious about my analysis of your writing from a long-ago teacher.

You ask if I have nostalgic memories ... most definitely! When one gets to be of the age of elders (how did that happen??), there are many chapters of memories! It is fun to be aware of the triggers to these memories ... a song, a movie, an aroma, a visual ... on and on.

Thank you for sending your cell# (impressed with your BTW code) ... one of these days we may be able to move our pen pal status to phone chats.

Thanks for thinking of me and making the special effort to mail the articles. I want to send you via modern mail (electronically speaking) a couple of note card covers a local artist/sculptress made reflecting her NY roots and her emotional connection to 9-11. She gives them as gifts to friends who know her work.

Hope the temperature has moderated in Cambridge. Hot and humid is the daily expectation for me and especially since we are at the peak of hurricane season. How did we survive before AC.... I know we did but ... that's nostalgia for you!

Take care.
Roz

From: RALPH
Sent: Monday, September 3, 2018 at 11:16 AM
To: Roz
Subject: Re: Your Posted Articles

Hi Roz,
Having a good holiday? I hope you're not "laboring" too much! Thanks for that wonderful response to the articles I sent, out of "Yankee Magazine". Not only what you had to say about the literary stuff, but so much of your other commentary. I know we could sit down and kill an evening, exchanging thoughts about our common interests.

I checked into the potter's work. She does some very intricate patterns with clay slip, reminds me of pottery my wife and I found in some of the studios in Wales when we were living in London. Other graphics on plates are charming too. Doing random driving through rural areas of New England, we ran across potters who had set up studios and had their sign up at the roadside, inviting visitors. It's always interesting to chat with them about how they got into ceramics, where they learned the craft, and their production.

September 3, 2018

Hi Roz,

Departure time is closing in on me,
so I want to get this into the post
box tomorrow morning.

These greetings are no big deal.
Coming up with ideas keeps my mind
active, and I enjoy the graphics.
Some are for my son and his wife.
Others for his girls. Some friends
are targeted too, like the one in NY
who is into theatrical stage design.
He got quite a bit of recognition
back in 2003 so I made note of
that. Another friend moved away
from Boston, and we were sorry
to see him go.

Who knows? One of these days
you may be on the receiving end.

Hoping all is well with you. I'll
probably be phoning you in a few
days. Stay close to the hurricane
shelter.

Ralph

Referring to my letter, your compliments about my handwriting are gratifying, but what I am more interested in is your "analysis" of the imagery. Do tell me what you see. When I was in grade school (everyone using pencils then) my classmates often taunted me about writing so dark. I suppose a Ticonderoga #2 was too soft for my heavy hand.

You referred to yourself as "a long-ago teacher." Now, now … a dedicated teacher never stops teaching! My father, who taught for 15 years in a rural school of 23 pupils, in his later years had heart problems. On one occasion, I was with him in his hospital room, and a man came in to visit. Interestingly, it was a former student of my father's, no doubt 65 years or older. The man said to my father, "Well I'm glad to see you again, Teacher Insinger, but I sure hate to see you laying here in this hospital", to which my father replied, "Not laying, Paul, say lying!" A teacher to the end!

Your follow-up email with the note card covers struck a sentimental note with me. The drawings are beautifully rendered. The one with the pile of debris, with a section of building wall standing erect in it, was specifically significant to me. That wall section appears to be part of a low building around the base of the Twin Towers. Those seven-story low buildings were the part of the project that I designed. I also worked on the entrance plaza, the observation deck on the top of the one tower, and most of the interiors of the indoor public spaces. The destruction was such a terrible waste!

Following your lead regarding note cards, pardon me for being so forthright and immodest, but I'm going to send you some copies of greeting cards I've made for family and friends on various occasions. Some are silly, others serious, but all of them appreciated by the recipients. All of it should provide a bit more insight about who I am.

Now I must go, having some shopping to do before I take to "the open road." I loved hearing from you, Roz, and soon on the road, I think we'll shift from emails to phone calls.

With a smile for you …
Ralph

. . .

From: Roz
Sent: Sunday, September 30, 2018 at 2:37 PM
To: RALPH
Subject: Smooth Reentry

Hi Ralph,
Am guessing you made it home late Tuesday night despite inclement challenges. Hopefully your re-entry after being away for weeks has been smooth and that you are back in your normal rhythm!

It was such fun talking and must say I smile to myself about how easy it is to communicate with you.

As the calendar turns to October, I think about changing leaves and the nip in the air that is autumn in New Hampshire and in Boston. The breathtaking colors (the joy of leaf peeping) and the crunch of the leaves on a long walk ... and adding another layer are always special remembered moments for me as I push the AC button up a notch in the temps of 90 in my autumn environment. C'est la vie ...

So, welcome home!
Roz

Sent from my iPhone

From: RALPH
Sent: Sunday, September 30, 2018 at 10:16 PM
To: Roz
Subject: Re: Smooth Reentry

Ahhh ... my best pen pal ... hi Roz.

Thank you for renewing our correspondence. And what a pleasure to be on a normal keyboard to access the words I need, instead of that iPhone pad where one of my fingers will strike about three letters, confounding the machine about which one I want to use.

You were correct that I drove late into the night to make it all the way home. I was determined to wake up in my own bed the next morning. My trip that beautiful first day out, it took me 11-1/2 hours down to Ohio; the same trip for my return, in a driving rain all the way back to Boston took me 15-1/2 hours. It was dreadful!

I think I may have called you from a rest area while on my way back. Or it could have been during a traffic stall on the expressway. I wouldn't dare chat while driving in that rain, also there were areas of fog in some of the mountainous regions of Pennsylvania.

The trees around here are still verdant and look like they will remain so for a few more weeks. Some shrubs though are already going yellow and red. The temperatures are descending now and I'm into a warmer wardrobe every day. I envy you your climate, wishing I could continue with the short-sleeve shirts and short pants, not to imply that my legs are so appealing.

My wife was always charmed when the first colored leaves fell. She'd be outdoors collecting the best specimens, take them inside and dutifully press them for a couple weeks of drying, then send them with a note to her friends in Japan, Hawaii, and Arizona. That always generated some return mail for her.

My son's wife's father is visiting from Paris now, and he's a pleasant fellow with whom I always enjoy talking (he speaks excellent English). Tomorrow morning I'll take him out for brunch. We should get a large omelet and all the extras because he likes to talk about some diverse subjects, and it could go on and on. I like breakfasts/brunches because the food choices are simple and not very filling. One can keep things going by simply keeping the coffee cup topped off!

Well, I found your message late this evening, so I apologize for not getting back to you sooner. You may not get this until the morning. However, you will have a note from an admirer with which to begin your day. I hope it's sunny and refreshing.

Thanks for your "welcome home". So nice to hear from you again.

Ralph

• • •

From: Roz
Sent: Wednesday, October 3, 2018 at 7:58 PM
To: RALPH
Subject: "Happy Distraction"

Hi Ralph,
I am resending this to you on the chance you did not receive it Monday
… it was fun writing it.

Greetings from the Toyota Service Dept Waiting Room! What a great
way to make time fly visiting with You. I am being a responsible and
dutiful car owner maintaining checkups to keep all parts moving in
perfect automotive sync …

Thinking about your response about not liking (not appealing or
relatable) the audiobook reader's voice and being sensitive to the
importance of this connection, reminded me of my experiences years
ago reading for the blind (print handicapped) on the radio in New
Orleans (WRBH) and the Metropolitan Ear for The Greater Washington
DC Area. I have many funny stories about the voice evaluations and the
selections of reading materials the reviewers chose for my voice … and
the listeners comments … best to share by phone or in person.

I actually have a copy of the CDs recorded of my reading Mitch Albom's
book *The Five People You Meet in Heaven* published in 2003 … most
famous for his book *Tuesday's with Morrie*. You might find it fun to
listen to passages one of these days…

Your breakfast/brunch today with your French in-law must have been
fascinating since you shared that he is a thinker with opinions. Wonder
what he thinks about the Senate Confirmation Hearings knowing that
our "government" makes constant international news. I was riveted
Thursday from the beginning until the very end of the session and
again Monday morning until 2pm. The emotional highs and lows defy
verbiage … Karen and I texted frequently … venting in disbelief or close
to tears. At one point we agreed we might move to Canada!

I loved reading about your wife being charmed with autumn leaves
… I used to collect the special ones (especially the brilliant red and
gold maples) when we would spend an October week in NH while my
husband was still working, to share with my staff in New Orleans who

had never experienced the season of fall in the Northeast. I remember drying the leaves and carrying the collection carefully in my briefcase to share for Thanksgiving tables.

Thanks for being a fun distraction! Until next time ... Take care.
Roz

Sent from my iPad

From: RALPH
Sent: Wednesday, October 3, 2018 at 10:53 PM
To: Roz
Subject: Re: "Happy Distraction"

Hi Roz,
Actually I did receive the first transmission of your email. But I have no complaint about getting a second printing ... it was amusing and witty, maybe even more enjoyable on second reading. I hope your Toyota service crew are as thoughtful and responsive as my Subaru pals here. They get me in and out so quickly I believed I wouldn't have enough time to get a message to you.

Having gotten to know a bit about you now and your characteristic pride in things, I would expect you to do the check ups, "to keep all parts moving in perfect automotive sync". (I love that expression). As for me, I'm more the dutiful body steward, maintaining check-ups to keep my body organs moving in perfect Homo sapien sync!

This week I'm in a crunch related to the church project I'm working on. Suddenly the builder for the remaining bit of work (the entrance canopy sheltering the front entry doors) notified us that he is preparing to start that work and wants to complete it in a couple weeks. So I've been spending my days and evenings checking the critical materials for the finishes and arranging to have them at the site "in sync" (again) with the schedule for completion. That's really why I didn't get a response to you when you wrote Monday. Tomorrow I'll be on the run again, looking for a supplier of molded fiberglass products such as we need.

Those Mitch Albom books you mentioned were good reads. My wife got them when they came out, and following her, I read them. I preferred *Tuesdays with Morrie*, I suppose due to Albom's real life genuine compassion for his mentor.

We're experiencing October rains now, all the markets are featuring stacks of pumpkins, and potted mums in bloom with lovely color choices, are tiered outside the entry doors. Corn stalks and straw bales are setting the scene for celebrating Halloween. We live on such a busy thoroughfare that parents don't seem to let their children roam here. We haven't had any trick-or-treaters for four or five years now, so we usually ate the basket of candy treats ourselves.

I'll just have to wait until Thanksgiving weekend ... maybe I'll get to treat two special women to lunch again. Thanks for remaining in touch. You are often on my mind.

Ralph

· · ·

From: Roz
Sent: Friday, October 5, 2018 at 9:52 AM
To: RALPH
Subject: Projects for the Betterment of Man-Womankind

Dear Homo sapien,
Kudos to you for giving of your talents and time to a church project that will be an improvement to the congregant well-being. Involvement in "projects" have so many benefits both for the doers and the receivers. It is personally gratifying to see a project through completion and know it was so worth doing.

Try to imagine the same autumnal display you mentioned in your locale at groceries in my neighborhood that acknowledge the consumer's seasonal dynamic in balmy temps that can still reach 90 degrees. Needless to say "trick or treaters" need not worry about "a wrap" diminishing their costume's impact.

Hope you will be feeling less pressured as "the project" gets underway and that there will be no glitches in the weeks of construction!

Happy weekend.
Roz

Sent from my iPad

From: RALPH
Sent: Monday, October 8, 2018 at 1:40 PM
To: Roz
Subject: Re: Projects for the Betterment of Man-Womankind

Hello Roz,

Writing to wish you a Happy Columbus Day. That's if you even celebrate it! New England is far away from where Ole Chris sailed, but most places here celebrate the day … anything to get a day off! I think it's taken advantage of. Consider for example that the medical offices close for the day. If you have a problem just go to the ER, despite the fact that the copay for an office visit is $10, and for the ER it's $100.

Columbus as we know, sailed into the Caribbean Islands, and according to the history books never stepped foot on the continent. In view of other lapses in history, should we believe that? Are you satisfied that Columbus didn't make a side trip around the Florida coast … maybe dropped in on Palm Beach Gardens? You may be living in a landmark community. You should be digging into the sand around your place, possibly finding some old Spanish swords, or arrowheads from the savages! (Oh dear, I guess I've gotten carried away, but it's a good excuse for writing to say hi).

Nothing has started today with my church project. The builders have taken the day off for the holiday. It's beautiful outdoors so they're missing an opportunity to accomplish something. I'm not complaining much because I have so many other things of my own to catch up with.

That's it for now. Stay out of that hot sun. Stay close to a tall, cold lemonade.

Ralph

From: Roz
Sent: Monday, October 8, 2018 at 4:04 PM
To: RALPH
Subject: "Columbus Day" Wishes!

What a treat to read your emails … even when they get into "a carried away zone"(your label not mine)! Tempting as it is not to call to chat, I don't want to miss your expository responses that make me smile! So, except for the mail delivery, retail sales and bank closures, Columbus

Day is normal in these parts ... students in school, doctors in their places and appointments scheduled as usual.

Other than sharing a pleasant interlude at the Art Museum, have we talked about our interests ... like music, theatre, ballet, opera, sports, travel???

Just thinking about our communication parameters and possible topics of interest ... curious?

Best as I can tell from history lessons, you are right Christopher did not step on Florida soil but it is thought, although some debate it ... that Ponce de Leon stepped on Florida soil and discovered "a water source thought to bring eternal youth " aka Fountain of Youth near St Augustine, on the east coast of Florida about 4 hours north of Palm Beach Gardens ... great info for trivial pursuit.

Til next time ...
Roz

• • •

From: RALPH
Sent: Sunday, October 14, 2018 at 4:39 PM
To: Roz
Subject: Re: "Columbus Day" Wishes!

Hi Roz,
Well, in a prescient moment you've exposed how entangled I am. I've lost our connection because the church project had me in its grip this past week, and I feel clasped in tentacles. Tomorrow the construction of the church entry canopy commences, and I've been dealing with several critical issues that need decisions. I am making progress. Meeting after the service this morning I got part of it under control, and tomorrow and beyond I should conclude the other details.

We are in a flurry here because we have set a date for celebrating the completion of the project (November 3) and that will sneak up on us like death!

Sorry I didn't get back to you on Columbus Day. I liked your inquiries ... it seems we may be going into a new range of topics to share ... music, cultural interests, travel. Yes, I'm curious about all those experiences.

When I listened to the wide coverage of "Michael" thrashing its way into the Florida panhandle, I was stricken, thinking about two wonderful younger friends of mine who have a home in Tallahassee. I took some time trying to reach them to know if by some miracle they escaped the damage. Late in the evening I found an email from them, both unharmed physically, returning to their home to find it essentially intact. It required some roof shingles to cover where some had blown away, but otherwise they were in good spirits. Ironically, there were other homes in the vicinity of my friends which suffered more severe damage. I like to believe their faith in the Almighty made the difference.

I'm happy to know that you were out of harm's way, and I pray that the hurricanes, now out to sea, will "cruise" for a while! I've got to go now ... other issues on my mind. But your note was sweet relief from a demanding day. Bless you.

Smiles for you,
Ralph

• • •

From: Roz
Sent: Saturday, October 27, 2018 at 9:55 AM
To: RALPH
Subject: Nor'easter and You

Hi Ralph,
My turn to ask about the weather you are having this weekend. Hope the inclement conflagration of the elements does not pose construction issues for The Project other than delay (your least favorite word) for the moment ... luckily it's weekend timing.

I am dealing with an aggravation that challenges my being too ... my AT&T Service (incoming calls on my house phone aka landline) is not functioning due to fiber optic wiring being laid interrupting service ... at least that's the latest verbiage/explanation I have been given. This is third time in the last two months of this inconvenience that requires my alerting family and friends to reach me on my cell. Annoying!!!!

Thank you, I feel better for the venting!! Adapting is a requirement to survival these days!

The news these last few days has been so distressing and then to learn yesterday that the many (13?) mailed "bombs" were sent from a disturbed man from south Florida (an hour away) was terrible. Praise to the FBI and its adept skills to solve the mystery quickly but still so upsetting for all involved not to mention our country!

Time to turn to creative expression today with soothing music playing and happy thoughts!

Hope you will weather the weekend in a warm and cozy environment!

Roz

Sent from my iPhone

From: RALPH
Sent: Sunday, October 28, 2018 at 4:58 PM
To: Roz
Subject: Re: Nor'easter and You

Hi Roz,
Your message was accessed rather late last night, but it was a welcome shot of adrenalin after a hectic day. Alas, I was too "drained" from the day's mix of activities, so I just had to get into bed. Sorry I didn't get a note back to you.

The weather was terrible ... ongoing rain (sometimes pouring), but I took off early to the local print shop and then to the church to deliver some drawings for the builder. We are behind due to earlier rainy weather, and the builder disappearing for a couple days to one of his other projects. He's trying to satisfy us and another client who is also trying to get his job completed before the snow flies. I've decided to simply hope for the best rather than give in to "the beast" in me!

From there I moved on to Brookline where my son lives. He and his wife both had meetings to attend most of the day, so I had offered helping, looking after my two granddaughters. That can be real punishment for an 83 year-old! The parents came home about 6 p.m. so we had a late dinner, after which I spent a bit more time with the girls while Mori and his wife did the clean-up. Then I took off for home and loved walking into a quiet orderly environment. One of those blessed occasions to which we seldom pay homage.

You're annoyed with our brave new electro-world? Of course you are. You and I are holding the fort to preserve some resemblance of a face-to-face touchy-feely world, but it's gradually slipping away from us.

I grant you your moment of venting ... after all I'm a certified venter myself!

Yes, the terrorism occurring these days is overwhelming. One would not suspect so much hate prevailed in our homeland today. But it's not hard to recognize who is fostering much of it. It's coming right from the top, just like Nazi Germany. I despair when seeing how much of the populace is swallowing such negativity. When Mori came home last night he asked if I had heard about the shootings at the synagogue in Pittsburgh. Of course I had not because I had heard no TV news nor internet reports. It was just devastating!

As for me right now, I'm weathering the weather. It has stopped raining since this morning but it is dreary and overcast. When naming the days someone slipped up ... this is hardly a sun-day! Nevertheless, after raising the thermostat a bit, having some time to relax with the newspaper and some calming music keeps me smiling.

That's something you do too! Stay as you are.
Ralph

• • •

From: Roz
Sent: Saturday, November 3, 2018 at 9:41 PM
To: RALPH
Subject: Congratulations ... Saturday Night Live!

Ralph,
If you are reading this after your Gala Event, you are breathing a happy sigh! Hope you are feeling the appreciation of all the friends and acquaintances who celebrated your architectural expertise and generous gift of self.

Just thinking about you and your success!
Roz

Sent from my iPhone

From: RALPH
Sent: Sunday, November 4, 2018 at 7:11 AM
To: Roz
Subject: Re: Congratulations … Saturday Night Live!

Dear Roz,
Yesterday as I reviewed some comments I prepared for my brief part in our evening dedication service, I thought about you. Intuitively I realized that you were probably thinking about me and wishing me well. And your email proved how well I've come to know you. Not only are you my muse, you're also that diminutive angel on my shoulder assuring me that all is well. Truly you are "dear Roz".

It was an uplifting evening. Many kind people who expressed their pleasure with what we have created. I've risen this morning feeling gratified and continuing on to this morning's service shortly. But I wanted to acknowledge your lovely note of understanding about what the evening was all about. I'll be in touch later to fill in the details.

Bless you.
Ralph

• • •

From: Roz
Sent: Tuesday, November 6, 2018 at 11:46 AM
To: RALPH
Subject: TODAY!

Hi Ralph,
Well, today has come and I am in "prayer mode" … hope/optimism springs eternal in the human heart. Sigh … .

In between media coverage in anticipation of tonight's numbers, I am distracting myself with "phase one" of my packing process for my departure to Boston 11/16. I am always challenged to travel with less as more. Sad to say, I am rarely successful if the trip extends longer than 3 days! Truly laughable … .

I was so pleased to read your email acknowledging the success of the November 3rd Happening! Nice to be less pressured!

Roz

Sent from my iPhone

From: RALPH
Sent: Tuesday, November 6, 2018 at 2:43 PM
To: Roz
Subject: Re: TODAY!

Back atcha, Roz,
I share your feelings about tonight's results, on tenterhooks* about the outcome of election day 2018. The only state I have no doubt about is right here … Massachusetts. The national media have gotten so cocksure* these final days running up to the election, apparently comfortable that the tide is moving in favor of the Dems taking over the House and maybe the Senate too. I'm holding my breath tonight.

Your designation of "phase one" as you begin packing, evoked laughter here. It ensures there will unquestionably be more to come! Pack as much as you want and take comfort in someone's revision of less and more … he said, "Less is a bore!"

I'm drawing a target on my calendar date 11/16, though I may have to wait until sometime after Thanksgiving to have lunch with you. I'm patient … a Roz at any other time will be as sweet!

The church celebration on November 3rd was a pleasure for all. The formal service and the dinner conversation later were sprinkled with anecdotes about the building project. It was lighthearted and amusing throughout. I'll reserve some of the proceedings for when we are together because right now I'm feeling drowsy and think I'd better settle for a nap. Forgive me for putting you on hold now, but I still have nine days to get back to you.

For now, I hope the evening goes your way, which I think is my way too. Will talk again soon.

Ralph
* archaic usage

• • •

From: Roz
Sent: Monday, November 12, 2018 at 6:37 PM
To: RALPH
Subject: From One Bird to Another!

Hi Ralph,
What a happy surprise to hear your phone message today when I returned home at 5:30 after a marathon day! Think it is perfect that you found the cartoon that confirms my invitation to you to visit me and the land of the swaying palms during the winter! Any sensible person of a seasoned age should escape wintry weather if possible … avoiding shivering, slipping and sliding, not to mention cold, wet (although beautiful snow when fresh fallen) snow, slush, shoveling, defrosting, etc. etc. etc. No worries, I will continue my tourism pitch "as time goes by"!

Suitcase perspective remains one stuffed bag with contents for 12 days! Still in the selecting/ rejecting phase hoping to move into final stage by Wednesday for Friday departure! Thank you for your interest/ curiosity. What a saga …

This week is very busy for me with meetings, book club, Culture Club and bridge. I relish quiet evenings to recoup, although this week has two dinners to attend. C'est la vie!

I am getting excited about spending time with the family on the Cape for Thanksgiving. The family decided to "vacation" together for the holiday in an Airbnb in Harwich (I am delighted to be included) … and time together in Allston prior to the Cape. So, new scenes await me … hope your schedule and plans will allow us to get together during my visit! Happy to chat by phone anytime.

Stay warm!
Roz

Sent from my iPad

• • •

From: Roz
Sent: Wednesday, November 21, 2018 at 8:06 AM
To: RALPH
Subject: inSIGHT Through Education

Dear FPP (favorite pen pal) aka Chef Raoul,
Thank you for a lovely evening ... Thank you for your honest and easy
conversation gifting me with so much to think about! Really was
special to view The Church, your neighborhood and to meet your
neighbors who clearly treasure you.

Wishing you and yours a Happy Thanksgiving as we count our blessings
and not the calories! Togetherness at holidays remind us of how much we
have to be grateful for as we remember our spouses in our hearts.

Hugs,
Roz

I am sending you a link I think you will find interesting.
Sent from my iPhone

From: RALPH
Sent: Wednesday, November 21, 2018 at 2:55 PM
To: Roz
Subject: Re: Thank You!

Good afternoon, Roz,
Looking at your 8:06 AM transmission, I'm impressed the way you were
up and online at that early hour. Well, I suppose if you're paying for a
house on the Cape it's prudent to quickly get a few local details out of
the way, then head south and settle in. At that hour I was still comfortably
between the sheets!

When I did arise it was so nice to find your message with those kind
thoughts. It was so easy last night to keep the conversation going with
you, and when I finally returned to my home I was somewhat stunned how
fleeting the hours had gone without much notice from me.

Your "favorite pen pal" acronym caught me off guard ... I see FPP so often,
because it's used to abbreviate my street name. Interesting to get a fresh
look at expressions we use.

Thanks for the link to the short video about "inSight". That's a significant program to socialize our young people away from intolerance and bigotry. It was shocking to look back at some of the imagery of brutality that was accepted in those Fascist years of WWII. How is it possible that such prejudice is getting started again?

On a better note, I'm expecting my Thanksgiving celebration to be a pleasant time with persons I like but only get to see every so often. The host is a winner with the food she prepares, so everyone will eat well, but you have it right, no counting calories!

Someone usually comes up with appropriate words to consider on a celebration day such as tomorrow. I read the following this morning which aligns so well with your words that we have so much to be grateful for.

"For the hands that tilled, for the hands that harvested, for the hands that processed, for the hands that transported, for the hands that stocked, for the hands that sold, for the hands that bought, for the hands that prepared, for the hands that will hold, for the Hand that made the hands, our hearts are forever grateful. Amen"

Friends like you are at the top of the list.
Ralph

• • •

From: Roz
Sent: Sunday, November 25, 2018 at 8:10 AM
To: RALPH
Subject: Collecting my Thoughts!

Taking a much needed breather ... Thought I would say "hello" on this Sunday Morning (everyone still sleeping or as you so poetically stated "enjoying being between the sheets") with raindrops falling and trees swaying happily in the windy warmer temps! The house is quiet and I can think.

Hope you've had a nice few days feeling the holiday spirit. I have been thinking a great deal about the many interesting and heartfelt thoughts we shared and note the humor that balanced some of the more serious revelations, particularly about our families. I am really amazed and then not so amazed at how easily we talked ...

Wishing you a happy day.
Roz

From: RALPH
Sent: Monday, November 26, 2018 at 12:08 AM
To: Roz
Subject: Re: Collecting my Thoughts!

Ohhhhhh ... Roz,
Taking a breather? What an enlightened idea. I feel like I've been on a merry-go-round since we had that delightful evening together. The hassle included preparing my contribution for the "round table" Thanksgiving dinner to which I'd been invited. On Friday I put some drawings together for one of the contractors to finish his work at the church, plus re-stocked my fridge which had dwindled to some basics (you know ... butter, sauces, pickles, jams,etc.). Yesterday morn I made a large apple tart to take to my son's for a diminutive 2nd turkey-fest in the afternoon with his family. (The tart was superb and is the favorite dessert of my granddaughters). Mori loves roast turkey and all that goes with it. I went early, to play with my granddaughter while Mori put everything together. Today of course was Sunday worship, so I finally got MY "breather", with the bonus that a group of us decided to go out to lunch after the service, tying up a table at the restaurant until 3:00 pm. Then I went home and relaxed. Sigh!

It wasn't until late this evening that I found your email. It was uplifting to read and I regret I didn't find it earlier.

Your message suggests to me that you haven't been a couch potato while at the Cape. I'm glad the temperature was somewhat better than here, and you apparently found things that captured your interest out of the house, or challenged your imagination while you were stuck indoors.

We did share some heartfelt thoughts that Tuesday evening we were together. That was the pleasure of the time we devoted to our deeper feelings regarding our personal lives and the attitudes we have about the wider world to which we're tethered. You make it so comfortable to talk with, and you have a lot to say. About humor ... yes, I think we both love laughter. I recognize now how I used to take myself too seriously, but I try not to anymore. We have much more to talk about, and I hope we can get on with it again soon.

When will you be back?
Ralph

From: Roz
Sent: Monday, November 26, 2018 at 7:54 AM
To: RALPH
Subject: The Brevity of Time!

Glad to know your days have been filled with good happenings, marathon and all! As for me, the Cape was very cold for the first couple of days but the Togetherness glow was warming.

Karen and I escaped to a movie we enjoyed very much Friday afternoon ... we saw "Green Book" based on a true story with a unique storyline. Saturday was a lovely day so we drove to Chatham Beach, walked the sand and captured a few "memory keepers" to view over time.

Chatham is a charming town and was very crowded with locals and visiting family enjoying the warmth and shopping. Yesterday was marathon football for some and reading "The New York Times" for me ... Now that the guys have returned home to work today, and leftovers have been dispersed to respective domiciles, thank goodness ... we women will spend today together in Hyannis before the predicted rains late this afternoon.

Sadly, we will return tomorrow to Lowell, and I fly home early Wednesday morning. My heart always feels heavy as I approach departure since being together with Karen and family is always special for me, no matter the locale. I am pleased knowing the family will come south to be with me sometime late December (depending on their respective schedules).

I am sad, too, that time for you and I to grow our friendship was so limited. With distance and traffic and busy schedules we were challenged to "make time happen". I hope you will seriously consider my invitation to experience my neck of the "woods" in these upcoming winter months where distance and climate are not an issue once the plane ride is accomplished. I promise the scene will be casual and relaxed in tropical surroundings (a variety of green and floral)!

I am so happy that we had our "Tuesday with Ralph/Roz" evening "getting to know each other" and thank you again for making it happen in such a lovely way. Can't help smiling thinking about the potpourri of topics so easily shared! And I have a much better sense of your physical surroundings thanks to your driving tour … so pleased to have this familiarity.

Take care of You!
Roz

Sent from my iPad

From: RALPH
Sent: Tuesday, November 27, 2018 at 12:22 PM
To: Roz
Subject: Re: The Brevity of Time!

Your comment about the good things surrounding Thanksgiving, regardless of the "marathon" that goes with it, was right on. Despite all the hustle, when the moment arrives to sit down to dinner in the company of good friends, it's a time of heartfelt abundance, materially and spiritually.

The Tuesday evening you and I shared provided much the same pleasure, except our time together went beyond chatter … it included an element of charm from you across the table. I do regret that the glow was disturbed every so often by the adjacent table of four! :-(Chatham is a nice town to stroll and browse. My wife and I always made a point of going there even if we were staying in a neighboring community. We saw so many things we liked, and at an earlier stage in our lives we probably would have purchased. But in our latter years we knew we had so much more than we needed and would simply dilute any pleasure we could gain, due to what we already possessed. As you strolled, I surely appreciate the pleasure you must have savored with Karen at your side. That you will be departing shortly does seem sudden. But the fact is time waits for no one. You've spent your days with your loved ones, with whom you truly don't get to spend enough time. That's what is important!

I've been fortunate being given an evening to share with you, and it was a delight. It's building a basis of understanding between us and begging for more time to enlarge on that, and I hope it will happen. You're very interesting, and I know there is a lot more stashed away in our life experiences to be exchanged for edification or just common interest.

I hope your days here will give you many happy memories, to fortify you until coming together again occurs. I am seriously considering the possibility of a trip to see you, maybe late January or early February. We'll be talking more about that.

Now you're under the pressure of getting everything done in preparation for your departure tomorrow. (Aren't you glad I didn't give you one of those huge fuzzy stuffed animals to take home with you?) I hope all is going well. I'll call you early this evening when I expect you'll try to relax a bit.

Remember ... take a deep breath now and then! BTW, thanks again for the picture you gave me.

Ralph

• • •

From: Roz
Sent: Tuesday, November 27, 2018 at 5:43 PM
To: RALPH
Subject: On A Mission!

Checkout AMC Loews Boston, 175 Tremont and AMC Assembly Row 12, 395 Artisan Way in Somerville showing "La Traviata" Saturday, December 15th at 12:55pm (3 hrs 30 mins in length). Tickets can be purchased in advance ($20-$22).

Think you may be able to select your seat when you purchase your ticket (this is the case for me which makes arrival at Showtime very civilized). My departure gift to You!

Know you are smiling!

Sent from my iPhone

From: RALPH
Sent: Tuesday, November 27, 2018 at 10:50 PM
To: Roz
Subject: Re: On A Mission!

Ah, Roz,
You're the best! My personal concierge! Thanks so much for taking time
on your final evening with the family to find the source of tickets I need.
I'll get down to AMC Loews Boston soon. That's the most conveniently
accessible theater by the T ... I don't want to deal with finding parking.

I'm wishing you safe travel and a wonderful reception from your friends
when you arrive home. That you'll have sunshine and warmth is a given!

Yep, I'm smiling!
Ralph

• • •

From: Roz
Sent: Thursday, November 29, 2018 at 9:56 PM
To: RALPH
Subject: Successful Re-entry!

Dear FPP,
Just in case you were wondering ... I have accomplished all the issues
that face "travelers return" from unpacking, sorting mail, paying bills,
modest grocerying and answering phone messages all in the cycle of 24
nonstop hours! Whew!

Yes, the weather is as it should be in this part of the world and as you
so aptly phrased it, my thoughts of my time in Boston and its environs
are constants of positivity and joy ... with time shared with you and
communications with and from you at the top of my list!

"Yep, I'm smiling!"

Too exhausted at this point to tackle any "think challenges" so suffice it
to say ... til next time!

Roz

From: RALPH
Sent: Saturday, December 1, 2018 at 1:05 PM
To: Roz
Subject: Re: Successful Re-entry!

Hi Roz,
Loved your subject line ... so appropriate for anything in space going back into Florida. So glad you survived it by way of a smooth landing, not plummeting to the ground like a Boeing "coconut"!

If you are like me, you're so happy to be back in your normal lifestyle ... for about a week ... then you wish you were away again, out circulating in some stimulating pocket of the world.

Disregard the "think challenges". Go out and smell the roses!
The best I can tell you is yesterday we completed the front of the church. The supporting spire and the gold cross atop were installed Thursday, and the ceiling of the canopy, plus assorted trim pieces were finished yesterday. Praise the Lord, it is amazing! The few who have seen it so far expressed their emotion about its deep spiritual significance to them. Personally, I'm humbled.

I'm putting some things together in an envelope and posting it to you today, just some minutiae that I found as I was purging some long-held files. Maybe will give you a bit more insight into who I am (or was).

There are a lot of emails waiting to be answered, but you were first. Now I'm cutting out to try to clear away the rest of my writing. Thanks for understanding ... I'll get back to you again soon.

You're gone, but not ever forgotten!
Ralph

. . .

From: Roz
Sent: Monday, December 3, 2018 at 7:32 AM
To: RALPH
Subject: Entry to My Street

Ralph,
At your advice to" go out and smell the roses", I snapped this for you
on my walk this morning. This is the vision I have each time I enter
and exit my street. Although this is not rose season, bougainvillea
and impatiens color my view at the moment. The stark difference of
December and its seasonal phenom of natural beauty is meant to entice
you as you experience Cambridge and the winter ... not subtle at all!

Happy Monday!
Roz

From: RALPH
Sent: Monday, December 3, 2018 at 8:56 AM
To: Roz
Subject: Re: Entry to My Street!

Good morning Roz,
From your timeline I see that I'm running an hour later than you. I'll
probably never catch up with you today.

Nevertheless, your message and photos are a marvelous introduction to
the day. The palms and bougainvillea are truly breathtaking, enough to
get me up, out of the house and down the street to feast my eyes. It's no
wonder you thrive on being there.

The envelope I put in the mail Saturday went Priority Mail, and I was told it
would be in your hands Tuesday. I hope the postal service lives up to that
commitment. Not as if it's a big deal, but I didn't want you holding your
breath as though the contents were a matter of life or death.

Your email this morning provokes me to begin looking at plane schedules
and flights south. You keep this up, and I'll be at your door before
Christmas! Thanks Roz for invigorating me today.

Ralph

PS - Here's a little tidbit from this morning's Boston Globe. The few lines say a lot ... sad isn't it?

What we mourn when we mourn President George H.W. Bush!
Bush is being widely hailed as a president of decency and integrity. How sad - and telling - that decency is now a standout quality in a president.

From: Roz
Sent: Wednesday, December 5, 2018 at 10:27 PM
To: RALPH
Subject: Just because ...

Dear Ralph,
Just because my day today was full of activities I decided to tape President George H.W. Bush's Funeral Service. Out to dinner tonight with a group of women who gather the first Wednesday of the month brought me home at 8:30 ... tired but resolved to be a responsible citizen, I turned on television to watch the ceremony of today. I was moved and touched by the courage and determination of our 41st President ... his far reaching leadership for our country and the world, the principled man of character and humor who won the hearts and respect of many and his abiding love of family. I was brought to tears so many times ... my one thought in reflection was that I wanted to email you, just because..

Roz

Sent from my iPad

From: RALPH
Sent: Thursday, December 6, 2018 at 6:50 AM
To: Roz
Subject: Re: Just because ...

Good morning, Kindred Spirit,
Our spirits must surely be entwined ... I also committed myself to watching the ceremony honoring President George H.W. Bush. Instinctively I believed you would watch as well, because I think I've recognized a vein of civic duty that is imbued in you. Kudos to you, Roz! You expressed yourself so beautifully.

Personally, I had a couple medical appointments yesterday morning which I would not give up. So I had concern about missing the TV coverage of the funeral. I was heartened when arriving home just before 11 a.m. to find the ceremonies were just beginning. The next two hours touched me deeply.

The man was revered by so many, not just for his Presidential accomplishments, but the manner in which he conducted his private life. He dedicated his entire life in service to his country, but never lost sight of his commitment to family and friends. He held on to his principles regarding our responsibilities in human relations.

The presentation was such a moving tribute. Jon Meacham spoke so eloquently. James Baker spoke so well with intimate information about their personal friendship, never concealing his admiration and gratitude, nor embarrassed to show his emotion. I thought the Bush's minister from their Houston church was remarkable in telling about his friendship, with details of the President's spiritual strength, his faith and love of God, humbling himself to the Almighty. (The minister reminded me of my own pastor).

It was significant to me that from time to time during the service, the TV crew editing the video imaging did well in selecting the best moments to focus on President Trump, bringing some clarity of the chasm between his destructive policies and the achievements of "41".

I understand your tears ... there were salient moments during which I wept too. I was humbled and feel no shame in revealing it. I know your heart too and am happy that we can mutually commiserate so perfectly. Our friendship is so special ... just because!

Ralph

From: Roz
Sent: Thursday, December 6, 2018 at 8:13 PM
To: RALPH
Subject: Your "Good Morning" email!

Dear Ralph,
I am really challenged to find the words to convey the warmth and happiness I felt reading your expressions this morning? Still boggles

my mind, despite the many times I read and reread your words how connected we seem to be ... despite the miles. Being "simpatico" is a rare happening ... and yet you surprise me over and over again with your special "way with words", unique expressions that articulate far beyond the email transmission, touching upon intuition and instinct ... "tis a puzzlement" ... a very nice puzzlement.

Trust your meeting this morning was interesting and meaningful. How lucky you are to have someone to talk to and to listen to who truly understands you and offers you intellectual gifts to savor and reflect upon. Mutually fortunate, as you describe for the two of you.

Been thinking about a couple of things to chat about when next we talk ... your experience in the armed services and your academic position at U of M. Would be happy to read your thoughts if you prefer emailing.

I am in a bit of a pressure cooker ... must do my reading assignment (like homework since I have procrastinated ... very unlike me!) for my Book Club Meeting Monday afternoon at my house. Must be at the top of my game hostessing and all! Fortunately, I am not the discussion leader ... know you are smiling!

Til next time.
Roz

From: RALPH
Sent: Friday, December 7, 2018 at 12:05 AM
To: Roz
Subject: Re: Your" Good Morning" email!

Dear Roz,
With reference to your Book Club meeting Monday, you said, "Fortunately I'm not the discussion leader." My brilliant cranial processor shot back instantly, "Well that's a pity because you are so qualified to be the leader." You think, and you inquire and take a 360 degree view of an issue to judge it intelligently. That's good sense. I'll bet as a teacher you were never comfortable with simple, forthright decisions. There's more than one way to evaluate circumstances. (For example, that 2 and 1 make 4!) Even if you are not the leader, I'm confident you personally can wring every bit of relevance out of the material under discussion.

In my writing, words often just pop into my mind and fit properly as I want them to. Then there are moments when I have a thought to express, but I just can't come up with the word or two that would give the thought clarity and brevity. That's when I resort to profanity! (Sorry, but what he says in Cambridge stays in Cambridge)! Your own writing since we started these exchanges has given me insight into creating a relationship. As I stated in the opening above, you nibble around a person or a subject or an idea and want to examine all of it. That develops into an understanding that improves your perspective or broadens your knowledge bank. I like a person who doesn't beat around the bush, asks pertinent questions (tactfully of course) which generates depth in the conversation. Thankfully, that's you.

Your suggestion suits me that we might talk about my life in the military, and/or what might be called my "ivory tower" academic experience. That could well expose you to boredom, or boor-dam. We can keep a pillow handy in case you want to snooze intermittently.

Have a lovely meeting with the Book Club. Beware of paper cuts from the dust jackets! It's been fun talking with you.

Ralph

From: Roz
Sent: Saturday, December 8, 2018 at 8:01 AM
To: RALPH
Subject: "What he says in Cambridge stays in Cambridge"

Your quote, aka "the Vegas quote", seemed to find a "sticking place" and coincidentally because this month's Book Club selection (*News of the World* by Paulette Jiles ... finished the book BTW) is about words as tools of communication and the reading of words for the sake of edification (and in this unique book's plot ... "livelihood").

Being curious, thank you Google, Urban Dictionary offers the following: profanity - a linguistic crutch for the inarticulate ... refers to offensive, irreligious behavior showing religious disrespect ... As I thought about this definition (although not Webster), I reached a personal acknowledgement, which to an extent reflects my personal growth over the years. As a child of the fifties, and "a good girl of respectable inclination", it goes without saying a curse word would not pass my lips. Fast forward into young adulthood and early motherhood (now a product of the sixties) ... dramatic change occurred, albeit gradually, due to an epiphany that saying "a certain kinda word" provided homeostasis to my existence. The freeing of expression that enlarged my vocabulary was a giggling, fun release, not a crutch. Suddenly, one syllable words that were at first whispered and then became audible absolutely communicated the real meaning meant to be conveyed (if only to myself at first).

So, in summary, to be genuine and authentic, the "off-color" labeled curse words of the profane nature definitely have a place in my communicative expression today! On the other hand, care must be taken to maintain equilibrium in usage and to select only the appropriate circumstances to say what you are really wanting to say!

So what "stays in Cambridge" may eventually find its way "out of Cambridge" ... just a thought.

Sent from my iPad

From: RALPH
Sent: Monday, December 10, 2018 at 2:50 PM
To: Roz
Subject: Re: "What he says in Cambridge stays in Cambridge"

Hi Roz,
In my judgment Urban Dictionary gives the correct definition . Profanity is a linguistic crutch for the inarticulate. It 's an affliction of those who are clumsy and impatient as well!

That you have progressed over the years to finding use for profanity occasionally, pleases me only in that I feel you and I are more closely attuned. Still, I appreciate your concern for caution regarding the circumstances of the moment when we choose to use such words.

My own use of the profane vocabulary, interestingly enough, is not targeted on others ... it's directed at myself. I get so furious about some stupid mistake, or some inept move I made, because I didn't keep my mind on something I was doing. Nevertheless it always pains me to realize I'm so susceptible to gutter language.

Now on a better note, thanks for notifying me that you've received the audio-book. After reading that, it struck me I better check my CD player in the car to be certain I didn't leave one disk in there. If your grandson is going to drive to California, he's going to need every one of those disks to fill the time frame.

Something I forgot to tell you in previous emails is that La Traviata is not showing at AMC Loews Boston. The management confirmed that when I called to check a second time. According to them that theater does not have the equipment to receive the HD presentations. Assembly Row does (sold out), Burlington does (sold out), and I've been trying to find out from South Bay Center but they are not showing it on their "menu" of shows. I'm quite disappointed to find that most of the theaters showing the HD presentations serve food during the show time. Do you find that in your area too? I think the odor of a burger and fries would not be fitting with a good opera performance. I'll keep checking for locations.

I've got to cut out now. Got some shopping to do. Tomorrow will be somewhat busy too. A couple of older friends from my church, who no longer drive, were concerned about getting to the wake and funeral of a dear friend of theirs. They usually have a relative available but not tomorrow. So I've volunteered to drive them to the mortuary, and wait for them. They're not sure about attending the interment at the cemetery, so we'll see how that goes. We've been having rather pleasant weather for mid-December, but if it drops again into the 20's I have no plans of standing at a grave site. I'll keep the car warm and wait.

Hoping all is well with you. I can imagine your preparation and restlessness ... waiting for the family's arrival. It will be a wonderful celebration, and you won't have me interrupting the festivities this time. The best to all of you.

Ralph

. . .

From: RALPH
Sent: Friday, December 14, 2018 at 10:51 AM
To: Roz
Subject: Brief update
Attachments: home_slideshow_01a.jpg

Good morning Roz,
Here we are on the threshold of 12/15, and I'm disappointed I won't get to attend Verdi's outstanding La Traviata tomorrow. I was still looking for available seating at a convenient cinema location when Mori asked for a favor. He and his wife have tickets for an afternoon choral performance and thought they had a babysitter too. Not so for the latter, and they were unable to find anyone else, so I'm coming to the rescue.

It's not an absolute loss. While searching for scheduled presentations of the opera, I saw several reprise showings next week, so I'll check for available tickets at one of those theaters. I'm really curious about attending one of these simulcast presentations.

Among other things, the church work is done (except finish painting, which must wait until Spring for warmer weather). So I'm having some loose time now to do other things. Have done some Christmas shopping for the girls, sent some goodies out to a few special friends, and working on a Christmas greeting to send to scattered friends here and abroad. I've got to show some Christmas spirit and put up a decorated tree for the girls' pleasure. They are so excited about awakening on December 25th and rushing to the gift bonanza beneath their Christmas tree.

Well, dear, the day is getting away from me so I'm going to leave you for a bit. I hope you are gaining enthusiasm as the days pass and take you closer to having your loved ones by your side again.

With thoughts of joy,
Ralph

From: Roz
Sent: Friday, December 14, 2018 at 6:46 PM
To: RALPH
Subject: Steve and Me 5/2018

Ralph,
Steve arrived this morning, and we have had a great day! We are off to
dinner now, but I would like to talk to my FPP. When is a good time
for you? Later tonight or tomorrow before you are off to care for your
favorite girls? Mentioned sending a pic of Steve and me in my last email
to you but stuff distracted me ... here we are just because ...

Roz

From: RALPH
Sent: Friday, December 14, 2018 at 7:52 PM
To: Roz
Subject: Re: Steve and Me 5/2018

Hi Roz,
So nice to hear from you again. Also, I welcome the picture of Steve,
which is helping me to know a bit about all your family. What a handsome
man and a towering fellow to be sure. It's not difficult to imagine your
pride and pleasure, having him with you during this festive season. You
are looking lovely and happy in that picture and giving Steve every reason
for pride too.

I just got back from Mori's a few minutes ago and found your note. I'd love
to talk with you. However, I still have to cook some dinner, do the clean-
up, and my battery has really run down from today's episode. To chat a bit
would truly go better tomorrow morning, and I know you'll understand. I
have to be back to Mori's at noon, so I'll be up early to do all my morning
prep. Then a call from you about 9 a.m. would be exhilarating. Does that
work for you?

Tell Steve I envy every minute he spends with you. It would be my
pleasure to meet him some day.

Ralph

• • •

From: RALPH
Sent: Sunday, December 16, 2018 at 11:11 PM
To: Roz
Subject: The Christmas package I sent you

Hi Roz,
Perhaps you haven't opened the gift box I sent to you. When you do open
it, I think you'll have a good laugh ... at my expense! (Let me entertain you!)
Hope the delights of the season are soaring crescendo now.

Joy to all of you,
Ralph

From: RALPH
Sent: Monday, December 17, 2018 at 10:33 AM
To: Roz
Subject: The address you need
Attachments: picture.jpg

Dear Roz,
Happy to get a few minutes to talk with you this morning.

Appreciate your being my "postwoman", picking up after my mistake!
Here's the address for my friends. IOU ... a 50 cent stamp, and a lot more!

:-) Thanks.
Ralph

The attached, if you haven't guessed it, is a pic of my two granddaughters,
after their Christmas pageant yesterday.

From: Roz
Sent: Monday, December 17, 2018 at 11:09 AM
To: RALPH
Subject: Postal Mission Accomplished

Your card has been posted! Btw, love talking to YOU whenever
... makes me smile!

The picture of your beautiful granddaughters is a wonderful moment in time that demands viewing often and with delight! Know you are filled with feelings of pride as their loving Grandfather!

Dedicated & Devoted "Postwoman"

Sent from my iPhone

From: RALPH
Sent: Monday, December 17, 2018 at 1:27 PM
To: Roz
Subject: Re: Postal Mission Accomplished

Ahhhhh, if only you were bringing MY mail every day!

From: Roz
Sent: Monday, December 17, 2018 at 2:22 PM
To: RALPH
Subject: Re: Postal Mission Accomplished

Ask Santa! You never know!

Sent from my iPhone

From: RALPH
Sent: Monday, December 17, 2018 at 3:11 PM,
To: Roz
Subject: Re: Postal Mission Accomplished

I'll do more than ask Santa ... I'll beg him!

From: Roz
Sent: Tuesday, December 18, 2018 at 11:01 PM
To: RALPH
Subject: Re: Postal Mission Accomplished On Roz

Greetings from the North Pole ... just an FYI your request is under review!

HO HO HO!!!

Sent from my iPhone

From: RALPH
Sent: Wednesday, December 19, 2018, 7:22 AM
To: Roz
Subject: Re: Postal Mission Accomplished

Good morning Roz,
My-o-my, you were late last night. Nice of you to close the day with a note to me. For once I was in bed before 9 p.m. Had a day of running around and dealing with some run-of-the-mill issues, besides the normal prep for the holidays, so I was rather run-down. (Did you notice I'm into hyphens today)? I've already been up for an hour and a half, now expecting to leave shortly for groceries. Must fill the fridge. Don't want to wait until later and run into the crowd at the market.

BTW did you get your greeting card that should have been in your gift box? My long-time friend said he put it in the mail to you the day he opened his box.

I hope Santa is in a merciful mood!
FPP

From: Roz
Sent: Wednesday, December 19, 2018 at 11:15 PM
To: RALPH
Subject: Mail Delivery Tomorrow?

Dear FPP,
Perhaps tomorrow will be "receiving day" for us … if your Holiday Dance Card has an open time to chat tomorrow night, I would like that very much. If you are otherwise involved, perhaps Friday? I imagine you are in demand with festivities of the Season while I have countdown "To Do" lists in anticipation of Karen and family's arrival Christmas Eve. Thankfully all gifts have been wrapped! Making good progress and am not feeling Bah Humbug yet! Hope you are having sweet dreams …

From: RALPH
Sent: Thursday, December 20, 2018 at 1:47 AM
To: Roz
Subject: Re: Mail Delivery Tomorrow?

From one FPP to another,
It was getting lonely here this time of night (morning), and then I found your delightful note. I don't have anything happening tomorrow night. I'm "out of demand" now, so I'd love to talk with you. Do you have an approximate time?

Sorry you won't have Karen with you until Monday. She must be working too hard! Or were all the earlier planes already fully booked? I know you'll love it when she's there. I'm pleased with your diligence with gift wrapping. Stay cool ... you have Bah Mitzvah, you don't get to do Bah Humbug!

Dear, I am not having "sweet dreams". It's sweet anticipation, until tomorrow night.

From: Roz
Sent: Thursday, December 20, 2018 at 7:58 AM
To: RALPH
Subject: Re: Mail Delivery Tomorrow?

Good grief!!! Not to diminish my happiness to read you this morning BUT ... seeing the 1:47 a.m. timing of" send" was a gasp! Hope you are "sleeping in" this morning to balance your renourishment of self ...

Karen en famille's arrival is based on work schedules ... driving not flying ... Jon and girlfriend already in Florida on the west coast working with his baseball coach (they will arrive sometime on Christmas Day) ... each departing on different days ... juggling moment to moment ... anything but calm and uncomplicated!!!

Yay, let's talk! Please call me anytime late afternoon or evening. I am "at home" today! Weather is supposed to get a bit grizzly as a rainy, stormy front moves east and then up to you ... sorry.

Later!

From: RALPH
Sent: Thursday, December 20, 2018 at 9:09 AM
To: Roz
Subject: Re: Mail Delivery Tomorrow?

It's clear there is hecticity (is there such a word)? in your holiday scheduling. Breathe deeply Roz. But it all culminates in a marvelous few days together with your dear ones.

I'll be delighted to call you, probably about 7 p.m. There are a couple of late afternoon appointments to take care of before the holiday hits, so I can't count on phoning this afternoon.

Make your list ... not for Santa ... your list of things we can share tonight!

Meanwhile take care.

From: Roz
Sent: Saturday, December 22, 2018 at 6:04 AM
To: RALPH
Subject: ?

USPS Tracking informs me that the package I "prioritized" to you was delivered yesterday afternoon at 2:21 pm "In/At" Mailbox. Do you have it? Hoping you do!

Sent from my iPad

From: RALPH
Sent: Saturday, December 22, 2018 at 8:01 AM
To: Roz
Subject: Re:?

Good morning Roz,
All the way home last night from my day-care stint with my granddaughters, my mind was occupied with whether your package would be waiting for me. As I drove in past the entrance porch I noticed nothing was there, leaving me wondering. But entering the house I felt the door nudging something, and there it was ... your Priority package. Fortunately my mail slot is large enough for a package like yours to pass through. So it was safe and dry (we had rainfall all day yesterday).

For something coming from you I couldn't wait, so I opened it right away and was really pleased to find the book by Jon Meacham. I admire him a lot, after having read his commentaries, heard him interviewed on TV, his participation in panel discussions and watched as he eulogized George H. W. Bush recently. Meacham is so sensitive, literate, and informed, with a lot to say. I'm truly pleased and grateful to you for this book Roz.

Nothing much else to report. I did catch up on some sleep last night. Early to bed and early to rise. Feeling renewed this morning and a good breakfast should condition me to get going. I'll be talking with you by phone next time. And I won't wait too long!

Ralph

• • •

From: RALPH
Sent: Friday, December 28, 2018 at 10:35 PM
To: Roz
Subject: Re: "A picture is worth … " 12/26/2018
Attachments: IMG_1248.jpg

Hi Roz,
Today was a charming day for my little family of five. They arranged for all of us to lunch together at my home. So from about 1 p.m. to 5 p.m. we dined on sushi and vegetables, fruit and cake and then moved to the living room to have our own little Christmas gift distribution.

On December 25th we were split because my granddaughter was with her mother, and the rest of us were in Andover for that big family dinner celebration. That's why we delayed our intimate little celebration until today, so all of us could be together. The girls were loving the second round of getting gifts. Among the things I gave each of them was a 4" x 6" picture frame with a picture of their Grandmother. Going through some photos recently I found a lovely image I'd taken of my wife and wanted each girl to have a copy for their bed table, so they would always keep her in memory.

Now to this email for you. When we dined that evening at Pulchinella, I showed you a wallet picture I carry of my wife, which was not a characteristic image of her. Because you have sent me a couple lovely pictures of you, including your husband, I want to show you a better snapshot of her. That's what I'm attaching tonight … the same picture my granddaughters just received. It's more indicative of the woman she was, and I wanted you to see that.

We're on the threshold of a new year. I hope this year fulfilled many of your dreams, and the coming year will continue that. Make the most of what's left of 2018.

With fond regard,
Ralph

From: Roz
Sent: Saturday, December 29, 2018 at 7:47 AM
To: RALPH
Subject: Reflections

Dear FPP,
Thank you for the beautiful picture of your wife. I am so pleased to know you want to share her image with me and to know how much a part of your life she continues to be just as my husband continues to be for me. Keeping our loved ones alive in our lives is so important and giving your granddaughters a special picture from You to be placed in a special place has lasting meaning they will come to love and appreciate. It was important for me to establish a living tribute to my husband which became (with the huge assistance from one of his former chief residents and fellow nephrology colleagues) "The JELF Foundation For Children's Health" associated with The American Society of Pediatric Nephrology. I wanted Karen to be involved with me, and we are both so gratified to know this small effort has seen (and continues to educationally benefit young Pediatric nephrologists) successful outcomes. The JELF scholarships are in their eighth year and contributing positively to Pediatrics.

Your Family Christmas Celebration yesterday sounds perfect with the five of you being together, festively focusing on each other with more presents to open - happiness! There is something to value in "intimacy" as you so aptly stated.

Now about "approaching the threshold of the new year" … I can honestly say there have been highlights and lowlights in 2018 for me. My family had a very challenging health scare this year with my younger grandson (will be 15 in January) but thankfully he is doing just fine now as a happy freshman in high school . That family dynamic definitely qualifies as a lowlight (not to mention the political scene and the state of the world) ... on the other hand, the highlights have been many ... among them my very special communication with my FPP these last five months! I am counting my many blessings as 12/31/2018 approaches! I am excited and positive about 2019 and all the "unknowns" to meet and befriend!

Sending A Happy New Year Hug to You!
Roz

Sent from my iPad

From: RALPH
Sent: Sunday, December 30, 2018 at 12:36 AM
To: Roz
Subject: Re: Reflections

Dear Roz,
There's no doubt in my mind that I've disappointed you tonight ... replying to your wonderful letter so late in the night. I'm sure you have gotten to bed by now. I am sorry for my delay.

I was out and about today, doing some banking, at the copy center, getting a few last minute (and late) New Year's greetings to a few friends, and packing a few things for my "sleepover" with my granddaughter. Rather trivial as I look back on it. Tired now, it's so tempting to hit the sack, but I cannot put off writing to you. If I don't get to you now, my involvement the next couple days will render me "incommunicado", and you'll write me off for good, I'm sure!

Tomorrow I will go to Mori's at noon to take the challenge of caring for my granddaughter overnight. They will head for the Cape, returning Monday evening. It's my gift to them for an intimate getaway for just themselves, and my granddaughter has gotten comfortable enough with me (we think) so it should work out.

I'm gratified by your response to the picture I sent. It seemed appropriate to send you an image of my wife posed comfortably, and attractively attired because I find that comparable to how you appear in your photos.

The two of you seem much alike, attractive, characteristically at ease in a crowd, accomplished and self-assured. You're magnetic to others around you.

You impress me deeply with what you've done to honor your husband's memory, while simultaneously bringing generous support to students aspiring to become pediatric nephrologists. The growth in that medical specialty "comes close to home" for our family. Mori's 3 year-old, daughter was born with a kidney defect which doctors suggested be watched for possible improvement. However, it didn't happen, so last year she had a surgical procedure and now seems to be fine.

Judging from the travel by your loved ones next week, going in all directions, it seems somewhat like your own family "diaspora". I pray for their safety with weather and traffic in the highways and flyways. There always seems to be a mass exodus when the holidays end. As you juggle arrivals and departures, I imagine you have a calendar that is well inked on those pertinent dates!

Your concern upon hearing about your grandson's health problem (or potential problem) must have stressed you out. What relief you surely felt when you found he was out of danger. I'm glad to know that he's doing well.

I share your pleasure of having found a special new friend this year. It's a joy that keeps on giving! The prospects look good for 2019 being even more joyful. A New Year's hug is a good start!

Ralph

• • •

January 3, 2019

Dear Roz,

Kinda late, but I'm writing to thank you for your Christmas gift ... the significant book by Jon Meacham, about how to resolve contentious issues in current times. Your instincts for pleasing others seem to be "right on"!

To reciprocate (not because I think I must, but because I want to) I'm enclosing an item for you. In a light-hearted moment just after finishing my dinner, an idea came to mind, so I sat down and worked on it. I hope it's good enough that you might enjoy it. You will also get to see what I ate for dinner!

As a bonus you're getting a couple other miscellaneous pieces, to give a bit more insight of my family, so engaging that I want to get up and out of bed every morning; also a poem that I told you about when we talked recently.

Know that I'm always thinking of you.

Ralph

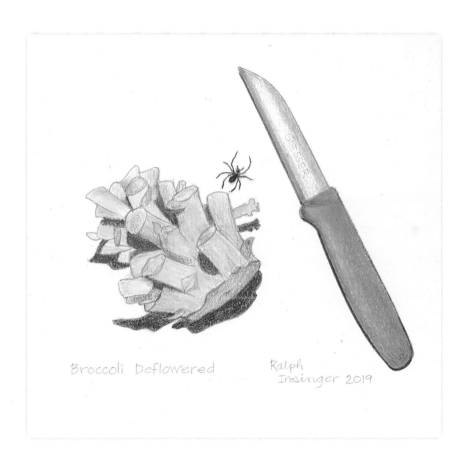

Broccoli Deflowered

Ralph
Insinger 2019

From: RALPH
Sent: Friday, January 4, 2019 at 12:04 AM
To: Roz
Subject: Re: My "Priority" to You!

Merci beaucoup! I'll check the theaters here to find where high definition Metropolitan Opera will be screened.

Regards,
Count Raoul of Saxony

From: Roz
Sent: Friday, January 4, 2019 at 8:26 AM
To: RALPH
Subject: Re: My "Priority" to You!

Dear Count,
Thank you for beginning my day with giggling laughter! How lucky we are to appreciate humor and share the gift of "phrasing words" that request a smiling response!

Laughter is curative and sustaining!
Your devoted Diva!

Sent from my iPhone

• • •

From: RALPH
Sent: Sunday, January 6, 2019 at 10:28 PM
To: Roz
Subject: Re: Thinking of you at this afternoon's performance!

Dear Roz,
Your photo work is certainly excellent. I'm delighted by the images you captured to show me something of what you attended. The program print was clear enough for me to read the compositions performed, so I went on-line to hear just what Enescu had composed. I didn't listen to the complete score, but what I did hear was melodic and somewhat light-hearted. For Romanians I would say that's admirable, possibly because the composer was relating to a national spirit back in the early 20th century, before the Russians

ran over the country. I checked into Strauss's suite from Der Rosenkavelier too, which seems to combine some lighter passages with other elements of emotionalism. In his Alpine Symphony I expect that, but I had thought Rosenkavelier was written as a more harmonious arrangement for opera.

I will say the roses at side-stage were an appropriate motif to accompany Strauss's piece.

Presumably you attended the performance with a friend or two, and that must have made it a delightful afternoon for each of you. Furthermore, with this evidence that you were thinking of me, you delighted me also. You're special! Sorry I'm so late in responding ... ! hope you are resting well.

Ralph

• • •

From: Roz
Date: Monday, January 7, 2019 at 6:24 PM
To: RALPH
Subject: Your INCREDIBLE Priority Contents!!

Ralph,
I am sitting silently in a chair I have not been able to move from nor do I wish to ... for fear the RALPH Spell will leave these moments.

I was excited to see your package in my mailbox an hour ago but was not prepared for its contents.

I am awash in your creativity, endearing sentiments and thoughtfulness that leave me speechless. Deep sighs seem to be the only elicited sounds in this beautiful silence.

I promise to be in touch to thank you appropriately for All that you have presented me with when I regain my sense of "other being." For now, please know I am deeply moved by your messages and your efforts.

Beyond beyond,
Roz

Sent from my iPhone

From: RALPH
Sent: Wednesday, January 9, 2019 at 4:04 PM
To: Roz
Subject: Karen's magic

Roz,
It's apparent that Karen made it back into your arms, then succeeded in transmitting your articulate reading of Gioia's poem. The sound of your voice was mellow, innately tinged with sentiment. The clarity of the recording was perfect, and upon finishing I savored a brief moment of sensuous assimilation, then I listened again. Talk about "what might have been"! To quote a highly regarded FPP of mine, the experience was "beyond beyond". I shall have to edge into a serious attempt at poetry ... specifically for you.

Charmed,
The other R in our relationship

PS - I've had a somewhat busy day, with essentially mundane pursuits. Spent the morning researching a workable lighting system with which we can spotlight the gold cross above our church. The lamp has to be bright enough to throw a narrow beam high enough to target the cross, without spillover that will illuminate brickwork, the edge of the roof, or nearby trees. I also want the fixture's box on the ground, compact enough to be mostly concealed by the planting around it. I think I've found what we require, now I'll have to discuss it with our electrical contractor.

Following all that I had lunch with a good friend, sort of my alter ego, off whom I bounce ideas or compare attitudes, which by the way has nothing to do with the cross-lighting I mentioned above. (I feel confident with that myself.)

Can't believe it's nearly 4 p.m. Got to go, love talking with you. Stay cool as you are ... and I don't mean temperature!

. . .

From: RALPH
Sent: Thursday, January 10, 2019 at 9:47 PM
To: Roz
Subject: Blueberry "picture"

Hi Roz
It's been a busy day. Regret not calling or writing all day. Thanks for your long and expressive email and your interest in night lighting. I love the range of distinctive features you take notice of ... things that exhilarate you.

Tomorrow I will be going to Mori's again to spend the afternoon with my younger granddaughter. We will have dinner altogether, then we'll all go to my older granddaughter's piano recital. When I go for dinner with them, I usually take a dessert they enjoy. So this afternoon I baked a blueberry pie ... first time ever! It looks good so I hope it tastes good too. I'm attaching a pic so you'll see my result. Doing it was nothing compared to writing this text.

Now I'm going to get offline before some "blue words" appear on screen. Hoping you and Karen continue having a fabulous time together.

I'm having sweet dreams and you?
Ralph

From: RALPH
Sent: Thursday, January 10, 2019 at 10:37 PM
To: Roz
Subject: Explanation of my previous message

My dear Roz,
How I wish I knew what I was doing with these hifalutin' hi-tech writing instruments! I had a pic of my pie on the iPhone, and I wanted to send that to you. So I presumed I had to send my text message with it ... and I laboriously sat and typed it into the iPhone. After some frustration, I got to the end of it, thinking I had really accomplished something. Then tapped "Send". Nothing on the screen changed, except a command "Edit" showed up on the margin. I tapped that and the screen eliminated all the text portion, and left my pie pic on screen. I thought I probably lost all the text, so I just gave up and decided to write you an email. When I got to my computer menu, curiously I clicked "Sent" and my iPhone text popped up, sent to your email address. I don't really understand why or how

this happened, but I hope you got it. (Mies van der Rohe, the prominent Bauhaus architect who immigrated to the USA when the Nazis began imprisoning modernists in the arts, used to defend his minimalist building designs by saying, "God is in the details!" That's how I'm explaining my message sending tonight.)

Back to smiling again now,
Ralph

From: Roz
Sent: Friday, January 11, 2019 at 8:53 AM
To: RALPH
Subject: YUMMY!

Dear Pastry Chef Raoul,
Your Blueberry Pie is beautiful pictorially perfect! Know all your lucky family will enjoy dessert (Titanically speaking, have dessert first)!

Culinarily Yours,
Roz

PS ... "less is more"

PPS ... you exist on a higher plane than I ... cause most of the time for me ... the "devil" is in the details ...

Sent from my iPhone

From: RALPH
Sent: Friday, January 11, 2019 at 10:16 AM
To: Roz
Subject: Re: YUMMY!

Dear Morning Star,
You are shining today ... your wit is on overload! Culinarily Yours ha-ha-ha!

And architecturally you're truly hip! Did you know Mies personally? I'll be treading cautiously as I pontificate into the future. Less IS more, so permit me to shut up now.

Thanks for your compliments regarding my pie. Glad you said "pictorially perfect". I'll report on how it went over with the girls after we do the "taste test".

Clever how you caught that item about God in the details.

Typically the devil does try to barge into our activities. However, when I'm involved culinarily, I keep him at bay, effectively relegating him strictly to eggs!

Do have a great day.
Chef Raoul (in service to the Countess of Saxony)

· · ·

From: RALPH
Sent: Sunday, January 13, 2019 at 9:55 AM
To: Roz
Subject: How long was it?

Good morning Diva,
Were you enraptured by Adriana Lecouvreur? I didn't find a theater with available seating ... besides, I wasn't too keen on spending 4 hours alone. I'd rather have you tell me about it anyway.

Thinking about you on my Sabbath.
Ralph

From: Roz
Sent: Sunday, January 13, 2019 at 11:33 AM
To: RALPH
Subject: Re: How long was it?

Dear Divo (learned yesterday the male title),
I look forward to sharing the three and a half hour Adriana/Count/ Princess rapturous triangle at your convenience!

Want to send you a few pics from this morning's walk-about with Karen at the Farmer's Market a couple of miles from home.

The Blueberry Pie Review? Later ...

Smiling knowing you are in my wavelength!
Guess Who

Sent from my iPhone

• • •

From: RALPH
Sent: Sunday, January 13, 2019 at 3:51 PM
To: Roz
Subject: Farmers Market in Palm Beach Gardens 1/13/2019

Dear patron,
Wonderful fungi and orchi at the market ... who was that peeking through the foliage?

Farmer-on-the-DELL

From: Roz
Sent: Sunday, January 13, 2019 at 4:08 PM
To: RALPH
Subject: Re: Farmers Market in Palm Beach Gardens 1/13/2019

The Orchid Man!
Karen and I saw "The Basis of Sex" (Ruth Bader Ginsburg story/movie) Friday ... really wonderful! Audience actually applauded the movie!!

And the Blueberry Pie review?

Respondent at the keyboard ...

From: RALPH
Sent: Sunday, January 13, 2019 at 4:35 PM
To: Roz
Subject: Re: How long was it?

Hi Roz,
Was holding my breath waiting to hear your report on the Met performance, then had to do "a long exhalation from the pain." But I know your enthusiastic response will keep until you're able to tell me.

The orchids you selected for your photo feature were extraordinary ... what elegant floral subjects with such rich colors!

I'm happy to tell you that the blueberry pie got rave reviews. I really baked it for the girls (who are never severe in judging) but the parents gave high marks for my baking talent. Now I'm waiting for my cordon bleu! I could bake one for you but they don't "travel" so well as Hazel Nut Babka. Maybe when I'm with you.

Ralph

From: RALPH
Sent: Sunday, January 13, 2019 at 4:42 PM
To: Roz
Subject: Re: Farmers Market in Palm Beach Gardens 1/13/2019

"The Basis of Sex", associated with RBG? Hmmmm, I'd never have thought that. But who am I to talk, at 83 years?

Dreaming Casanova

From: Roz
Sent: Sunday, January 13, 2019 at 4:48 PM
To: RALPH
Subject: Re: Farmers Market in Palm Beach Gardens 1/13/2019

My oops ... "ON THE BASIS OF SEX" ... legalese, legislative policy, gender equality ... saving commentary for conversation re: dreaming!!!!

The pictures of your girls are soooo beautiful! Can we talk tonight? Time?

Sent from my iPhone

From: RALPH
Sent: Sunday, January 13, 2019 at 4:53 PM
To: Roz
Subject: Re: Farmers Market in Palm Beach Gardens 1/13/2019

Talk tonight ... yes. How about any time after 7 pm?

From: Roz
Sent: Monday, January 14, 2019 at 9:20 AM
To: RALPH
Subject: Conversation Musings

Good morning,
It is intriguing to me that once we say "goodbye" as we close a phone conversation that our communication does not end for me ... matter of fact, I found myself thinking about an evening ice cream outing as a youngster in St Louis wondering if you ever experienced this ... going to the Pevely Dairy in the evenings watching the colorful fountains of water shooting in the air as one licked a plain cone (the only choice in olden days) ...
Once our phone communiques end I seem to have subsequent conversations in my head about thoughts you mention ... reflections, emotional revisits, intellectual juggling, keen interest, positive feelings ... curious to know more ... hmmm.

Non edible Food for thought.

Lots of dots (apologies for my many fill in the blank spaces this Monday morning).

Oh well, another cup of coffee.

Happy Monday!
Roz

Sent from my iPhone

From: RALPH
Sent: Monday, January 14, 2019 at 6:51 PM
To: Roz
Subject: Re: Conversation Musings

Hi Roz,
"Good morning" got away from me, so I'm switching to good evening. I was charmed to have your note as a send-off for my early trip into Boston this morning. Ugh! Except that I reflected on our conversation from last

night. It was as you stated, subsequent conversations in my head. For me that personal hour we shared was so nice, but went so quickly.

Those olden days you mentioned were golden days! Yes, I was taken for ice cream treats several times during the summer months. Not at Pevely Dairy, but in my hometown, St. Charles. Our town had a dairy that produced excellent ice cream and various organizations would do a fund-raiser promoted as an ice cream social, serving outside in a park or on a church lawn. Cones or cups were offered, and my parents liked ice cream as much as my sister and me. After a simple dinner, my folks would take us for dessert at those ice cream socials. How endearing that was.

I love your casual manner of telling it as it comes into your mind ... dots and all. It all goes so well with a cuppa joe! I hope the rest of your day was equally gratifying.

Now I'm going down for a quick bite for dinner, then will settle into the cushions and continue my reading with Jon Meacham.

Bless you for taking me there.
Ralph

• • •

From: Roz
Sent: Thursday, January 17, 2019 at 12:06 PM
To: RALPH
Subject: Drum Roll Please!

Hope you approve of my frame selection for My Smilemaker!
I am so delighted! Now the dilemma is to find my original art piece's new home! Smiling!

From: RALPH
Sent: Thursday, January 17, 2019 at 12:32 PM
To: Roz
Subject: Re: Drum Roll Please!

Drum Roll indeed! And bring out the trumpets! The work looks so good in that frame ... an ideal selection. Seeing the piece again, but now properly framed and secured, it looks so much better than when it went to you.

I'm so glad you enjoy it. The frame appears to have eased edges which I find to be an appropriate feature for this drawing. Kudos to you regarding your sensitive judgment.

My admiration to you,
Ralph

PS - You clearly have a fine framing shop. Such careful and neat winding of the wire suspension, and frame pads to keep it plumb against the wall. Last but not least, to leave the provenance exposed. If you do want to have the back of the frame covered with kraft paper for dust protection, photocopy the data label first and then glue it on the kraft paper. The original label will remain there for posterity :)

From: Roz
Sent: Thursday, January 17, 2019 at 1:34 PM
To: RALPH
Subject: Drum Roll Please!

I am pleased that you are pleased! Looks like a kitchen wall will be the display setting ... dilemma as to which placement I prefer. Limited options for best viewing ... stay tuned.

PS ... have used this framer since my arrival in Palm Beach Gardens (PBG) eleven and a half years ago. She knows my taste and eye for detail ... she was charmed by your artful expression! No stories accompanied the piece other than it was a gift from a special friend. She may think you are a good critic! Giggle giggle.
...

Sent from my iPad

From: Roz
Sent: Thursday, January 17, 2019 at 1:46 PM
To: RALPH
Subject: Drum Roll Please!

Meant "food critic" ... ugh!

Sent from my iPad

From: RALPH
Sent: Thursday, January 17, 2019 at 2:32 PM
To: Roz
Subject: Re: Drum Roll Please!

"good critic" ... "food critic" ... if you're around me very long you'll find that I definitely do criticize! It's something I must work on.

•   •   •

From: Roz
Sent: Saturday, January 19, 2019 at 8:09 AM
To: RALPH
Subject: Morning of Anticipation!

Morning Ralph,
Thinking about you as the snow/sleet/rain/ice/snow/rain precipitations move in Boston's direction! Tuned into your weather. Also sharing your concern about your property leak in these elements and the conundrum you are facing regarding repair (feeling frustrated and helpless). Oh dear ... not a happy scenario on several fronts (meteorologically speaking).

However, on a happy note, my Deflowered Broccoli (DF) is hanging in its place and reminds me of You and makes me smile so I am sharing positivity with You!

As you hunker down to be dry and warm know that I am only a phone call away and I promise not to mention my weather!

Roz

Sent from my iPad

From: RALPH
Sent: Saturday, January 19, 2019 at 10:15 AM
To: Roz
Subject: Re: Morning of Anticipation!

Good morning to you Roz,
You certainly have the predicted weather attack well documented. Seeing it all in that sequence, I am beginning to shudder! Just a simple

blanket of crystalline flakes, like manna from on high, gives me no concern, but I'm not so casual about rain, sleet and hail. I'm glad to have a garage to safeguard my Subaru.

The roof leak at my condo is now a thing of the past. Thursday I was notified that the contractor was on the job, and the repairs would be done by the end of the day. Later in the afternoon I received a call that the work was completed. The sudden call to action may relate to a letter I finally wrote to the property manager responsible for such property maintenance, with a copy to the company's CEO. The details about the manager's inexplicable poor performance were clearly stated and may have stirred up the powers that be. I guess we'll never know, but the main thing is the work got done.

I was confident you would place DB in a select location, radiating my spiritual presence (ha-ha). You, on the other hand, seem to overreach the ether, making you spiritually here with me each day. Nevertheless, thanks for keeping the phone line open too.

Don't stop smiling ... I won't.
Ralph

From: RALPH
Sent: Sunday, January 20, 2019 at 8:36 AM
To: Roz
Subject: re: Morning of Anticipation!

Good morning Roz,
Just as they said, we got 5″ of snow and now it's raining. Such a mess!

It was snowing very lightly when I slid into bed at 10 p.m. Awaking at 3:30, there still were cars moving on the parkway, and I could see the snow was about 3″ deep. At 5 a.m. the dripping sound informed me that it was raining.

The rain encouraged me to get up and get outdoors, to remove the deep pile of snow the plows had pushed into my driveway at the curb-cut. That was about 15″ when I started to shovel, and the top few inches was very wet and heavy. I cleared the curb-cut, then went to get my car from the garage and made my getaway. My driveway was still covered with snow but, my Subaru went right through it. (By now am I beginning to sound like my automotive friend who did the brakes on his van and installed a new front spindle on the truck? Sorry for getting carried away about my duties this morning).

Late last night Calvin sent an email to all the church members, cancelling today's service. We'll be worshiping at home instead.

Now that the important things are taken care of, I'm going to have some breakfast. I'll be thinking of all of you doing the same ... and I'll be smiling.

Ralph

From: Roz
Sent: Sunday, January 20, 2019 at 11:04 AM
To: RALPH
Subject: re: Morning of Anticipation!

Dear Master of the Manor,
Sounds like you have tended to all necessities presented to you (even in the wee hours of the morning) from elements beyond your control! You clearly are experienced in anticipatory and realities of weather phenoms (not your first rodeo) and are nestled now in the warmth of your home! When temps here drop into the 50's my "go to" weather-man announces a "snuggle alert". Enjoy!

Blessings to Calvin for caring for his flock safeguarding you/ congregants from any physical challenges.

My day today has been orchestrated by the play-off football games (Saints at 3:05 and Patriots 6:40) ... my son just called to say he and my grandson are on their way to the New Orleans Superdome with lucky Saints tickets in hand (they will surely have laryngitis by the end of the game)!

I am in charge of snacks and cheerleading for the family teams on this home front.

Last night I went with friends to see the extraordinary Miami City Ballet Performance (I have season tickets with several friends for the four performances at the Kravis Center for the Performing Arts in West Palm Beach). Last night the program was two ballets. The first was "DANCES At A GATHERING" choreographed by Jerome Robbins to piano music by Chopin and BRAHMS/HANDEL choreographed by Jerome Robbins and Twyla Tharp to music by Brahms. Classical and beautiful!

To be fair, today the weather here is cloudy (after early morning hours of rain ahead of a cool front) and will be grey and windy in sympatico from me to you!

Smiles ...
Mistress of the Casa

Sent from my iPhone

• • •

From: RALPH
Sent: Sunday, January 20, 2019 at 5:45 PM
To: Roz
Subject: Brrrrrrr ... .

Dear Mistress,
Without a doubt you are the Mistress with the Mostest! What a warm feeling I had when I saw that you'd written. Your words were gracious, a "tonic" surpassing a draught of hot spiced wine. It renewed me after an hour behind my shovel. (I realize you are not a wine drinker anymore, nor am I, but my wife and I, on a chilling evening often had a glass together in front of our crackling fireplace).

Just shortly ago I came inside again, after an hour and a half of more shoveling. The snow is saturated by rain now, so with 20 degrees F the snow layer is turning into thick ice. I wanted to get the pavement clear before that happened on my property. Tomorrow the Bruins will be able to play hockey all over Boston.

I knew you would catch on to that item about Pastor Calvin. He is so cognizant of conditions that threaten the elderly, and we do have quite a few older members.

Here I am at the computer, taking no notice of how your beloved Saints are doing. Are they carrying the game so far? It must be a thrill for your grandson to get to go to the stadium for the game. That must have taken a chunk out of Steve's wallet.

My personal choice for paid performance leans more to ballet than football. So, I envy your attendance last night. My wife engaged me in ballet. She was captivated by both modern and classical, so I always joined her in watching and became absorbed in the performances too. Still take time out for a broadcast performance when I see it on PBS programming, but it has been a long time since we attended a ticketed performance. I have hopes for seeing more in the future ... featuring my granddaughter. The youngest was smitten by a performance of "The Nutcracker", which she saw staged this Christmas season in Boston. Now she has tights, a tutu, and slippers, and she loves to dance for me. She's agile and rather graceful with arm extensions and the flexing of her fingers. Lovely to watch.

You are probably still watching the Saints. Are you on the edge of your seats ... what's the score? I'll go downstairs and check. I'm getting hungry anyway.

Blood pressure's normal ... heart rate stable. Nevertheless, I'm staying inside now. No more shoveling! Also, I better not watch the Patriots. That could excite me too much. I don't think they're favored over the Chargers.

Enjoy your family circle but don't eat too many of those chips and wings! Will talk to you again soon.

From: Roz
Sent: Sunday, January 20, 2019 at 8:38 PM
To: RALPH
Subject: re: Brrrrrrr ... .

Dear Iron Man,
So relieved to know your BP and heart rate are good, as in beating in perfect rhythm having given yourself a definite cardiac stress test this morning AND this afternoon. Shoveling heavy snow (ice laden to boot) is not for the faint of heart ... very impressive!

Sadly, my cardiac stress test did not have a positive outcome for the Saints!! So sorry for Steve and my grandson who are huge fans as is the city of New Orleans! Really looked like the Saints would be a shoo-in ... moods will be grim for the next few days. Fortunately, Steve's boss gave him tickets, knowing how much my grandson would enjoy being among "the faithful" up close and personal. Must confess I have little enthusiasm for the Patriots game but must be loyal and present in the moment.

Hope I successfully forwarded some internet ballet footage of moments I loved watching last night. I can picture your beautiful granddaughter in her leotard and tutu pirouetting for you. Delicious moments to cherish!

The plummeting temps in your neighborhood overnight and tomorrow are scary. Please take care! Sending warm thoughts your way ...

Feeling guilty in the temperate zone!
Roz

Sent from my iPad

From: RALPH
Sent: Monday, January 21, 2019 at 1:26 PM
To: Roz
Subject: re: Brrrrrrr ... .

Dear Roz,
You always have such upbeat openings to your messages ... it pains me to have to send my regrets to you about the Saints' game yesterday. It and the Patriots game were cliffhangers, but luck was with the Pats ... getting the call on the coin toss (especially with Brady calling the shots) really gave them an advantage. I'm blown away at times when I see what can be accomplished on the gridiron in just 39 seconds!

The ballet programming you sent was wonderful. Not only for reference to what you watched and where you attended, but the link afforded trailers of various performances, and some were select portions of a series of ballets, some of which run 20 - 30 minutes. Such poise and grace. One was a beautiful prelude to spreading myself between the sheets and dreamily submitting to sleep.

Awaking this morning to Cambridge's 3 degrees F quickly transported me mentally to your "temperate zone." Your warm thoughts brought me warm feelings. Thanks for your boost ... I am taking care ... I know when to pull back!

Heartily yours,
Ralph

• • •

From: Roz
Sent: Tuesday, January 22, 2019 at 3:27 PM
To: Ralph
Subject: Cup of Tea, Supreme Hazelnut Babka and You!

Thank you, Ralph, for the special afternoon treat! I will share your gift but am the first to taste the Babka as my son-in-law is working via phone and Karen is working at the gym ... my grandson is at the field, and I am enjoying Teatime!

Seems only appropriate to write the lyrics to you that were humming in my head early this morning for no "apparent reason" but seems to have found meaning now ...

"Getting to know you
Getting to know all about you.
Getting to like you
Getting to hope you like me.
Getting know you
Putting it my way but nicely
You are precisely my cup of tea.
Getting to know you
Getting to feel free and easy
When I am with you
Getting to know what to say.
Haven't you noticed
Suddenly I'm bright and breezy
Because of all the beautiful and new
Things I'm learning about you
Day by day."

Sent from my iPhone

From: RALPH
Sent: Tuesday, January 22, 2019 at 5:45 PM
To: Roz
Subject: Re: Cup of Tea, Supreme Hazelnut Babka and You!

Hi Roz,
Tea and Babka ... sounds like a good combination. I hope the hazelnut
babka is a success. There is so much chocolate babka that I thought a
variation would be nice. Do you take a little afternoon break for tea or
coffee often? I do it now and then, finding that it mildly recharges me, and
I like that. Otherwise, I'll take a nap.

You are much like me getting hooked on a tune early in the morning. I lie
awake for a while before rising and a simple song comes to mind. Then
I'm addicted with the music, repeating and repeating in my head all day.
One I remember from a couple days ago, from the Beatles, "Woman,
please let me explain, I never meant to cause you sorrow or pain ... "! As
you stated about GTKY, the words seem to have found meaning now. The
music of GTKY is so pleasantly lilting and spirited too.

This morning before starting to prepare breakfast, I put a CD in the stereo
... a series of adagios with a tempo that would get me started gently. As
the first track began, the music seemed unfamiliar with the opening bars
but then with the lovely orchestral string background, the delicate sounds
of the bass and harp took precedence. It was Bach's "Air For G String",
an arrangement so fluid and clear that it stopped me and overwhelmed
me ... so beautiful that it made me teary -eyed. Can you imagine such a
thing? I just waited until it was completed ... so touched by it . That's what
I like about opera. Emotion expressed in the music goes right to the heart!
Despite the ubiquitous snow, the postman did come today, and he took
some letters from me. Hmmmm, do you think there might have been
something in there for you?

Loving you for getting to know me!
Ralph

• • •

From: Roz
Sent: Wednesday, January 23, 2019 at 6:47 AM
To: RALPH
Subject: "Renaissance Man"

In a mind boggling moment, I realized that you, Ralph, are a Renaissance Man! As I reread (with less emotion and more rational thinking) your yesterday's email, it was clear to me that you wrote touchingly about Bach, expressed the meaningful effect of Opera, reflected about The Beatles lyrics, acknowledged a Broadway moment, discussed your rationale of a culinary gift selection AND ... add to this email expression your extraordinary list of personal achievements, among them visual design and construction, creative expressions both artistically and narratively, cooking and baking feats, gardening and beautification of your surroundings, snow shoveling under challenging circumstances, wonder at football dynamics, delight in ballet and love of classical music, travel curiosity, literary and poetic appreciation, strength of spiritual study and observance, deep love of family and reverence to long standing friendships, humanistic approach to life, a clever and charming sense of humor and the capacity to self reflect ... really Awesome!! But can you dance?

Your humbled FPP

Sent from my iPad

From: RALPH
Sent: Wednesday, January 23, 2019 at 11:56 AM
To: Roz
Subject: Re: "Renaissance Man"

Good morning Roz,
You are so gracious in judging who/what I am. That is such a wide-ranging set of observations, and coming from you, one whose point of view I deeply respect and value, I feel good about it. I'm more grateful than you can imagine. Notwithstanding, for truth and balance I have to tell you that I'm still rough around the edges. I'm pleased to have had my rural upbringing, simple and modest, more mundane than sublime. But I continue to learn about the elements of cultural richness and take pleasure in exploring the unfamiliar, for enlightenment or even mere enchantment. I'm not a social climber ... but I have enjoyed the company

of informed people who are far ahead of me. Now I've crossed paths with you, one who sharpens my interest in so many things that I (for the most part) had decided are not so important anymore. I love that you are nudging me ... that more is more! You are more than my muse. I believe there are moments you're touching my soul.

Your final question had me LOL! Can I dance? Yes, in a manner of speaking (and a manner of movement). In high school, as I began dating I realized I had to be able to dance. Without lessons, I did have a natural waltzy response to the music. Some young women just weren't with me, but a few were perfectly responsive to my moves. So I survived but I'm not into today's fast-moving physical style of livin' the rhythm!

Any more questions??????

Luv yuh Roz.
No Fred Astaire

. . .

From: Roz
Sent: Wednesday, January 23, 2019 at 9:22 PM
To: RALPH
Subject: Repopulating!

Just back from taking the family to dinner and want you to know I am having a private smile thinking about our phone visit! The slightest thought that you really will venture south is a potential collection of "post-its" of ideas!!! Must go into modest tour guide mode allowing for limitless talk time in the itinerary! Questionnaire underway ...

Will let you know my office hours as Swaying Palms are put on alert!

FPP

Sent from my iPhone

From: RALPH
Sent: Saturday, January 26, 2019 at 8:44 AM
To: Roz
Subject: Re: Repopulating!

Good morning Roz,
Reviewing your messages from the past week, I've found the attached which has gone without response. Tsk,tsk ... how inept of me. Forgive my insensitivity! You wrote so glowingly about how "sweet" it will be to get together, and your modus for organizing the myriad opportunities available to make my visit a resounding success. Love your enthusiasm.

I agree too with what you said about talk-time ... not a moment wasted as we spend time gadding about in places near and far. I'm certain you have so many stories to relate about your own discoveries since you moved down there.

Office hours be damned. My perception is "The Doctor Is In" sign is always up!

Hoping your day has begun well. I know you'll be cramming all you can into the time remaining with Karen. I must get moving too, having a lot of less-important running around to do today.

Bless you in all you are doing. Be safe!
Ralph

• • •

From: Roz
Sent: Saturday, January 26, 2019 at 11:50 AM
To: RALPH
Subject: Best Mother Daughter Therapy

Good Saturday morning to You,
Must have felt my wondering thoughts about your "tsk tsk" ... put worry aside, assumed you had a busy schedule and focused on winding down days with family. My grandson is on his way to New Orleans (departed late yesterday) where he will spend tonight at Steve's and celebrate my younger grandson's 15th birthday tomorrow before heading west to cross the big state of Texas. The driving journey will bring him to Palm

Springs, California by Friday. Karen will depart tomorrow so today we will focus on her and Shopping Therapy!

Best way to laugh together as Mother purchases for Daughter spaced between lunch, a movie and dinner. Full day ahead! We always love the exhausted feeling at the end of our marathons!

I am not happy about Karen driving the days alone (I offered to accompany her, but she is adamant that she will be fine and has done this long drive multiple times) ... she stays in touch as she maintains her "road warrior" reputation thanks to phone connectivity and audio books . Parents will be parents no matter what!!!! Although today is a cloudy, lightly rainy day, I am keeping sunny thoughts and looking to future plans. Wishing you sunny thoughts, too.

No Ginger Rogers

Sent from my iPad

From: RALPH
Sent: Saturday, January 26, 2019 at 3:05 PM
To: Roz
Subject: Re: Best Mother Daughter Therapy

SHALL WE DANCE?
No Ginger Rogers and no Fred Astaire,
No one noticed we're an exceptional pair.
No drag on the floor, no fear about flair,
No wasted motion, it should make people stare.
No admiration ... doesn't anyone care?
No wonder, I guess we were not aware ...
No one took notice cause we sat tight in our chair.
(From the diary of an Arthur Murray reject)

• • •

From: Roz
Sent: Saturday, January 26, 2019 at 4:01 PM
To: RALPH
Subject: Re: Best Laid Plans ...

Although a bit teary eyed, I know that our decision that Karen depart this afternoon rather tomorrow morning is in her best and safest interest. The updated prediction of heavy rains and possible tornadoes tomorrow for this area and north in Florida (coming across the gulf) forced us to abruptly change our Mother/Daughter plans for today!! Boo hoo ...

Fortunately for me, reading an Arthur Murray's Diary entry reject made me smile (relatable) as did the arrival of the birds nesting with the preponderance of that one "extra piece" ... how often have I been faced with an extra screw or bolt that creates a quandary for the inexperienced putting pieces together (a child's toy, a kitchen gizmo, heaven forbid an electronic assembly)! Can put one into a dither!

Is it commonplace for an architect to be "out on a limb"? Really? Usually, one observes the architect to be visionary and creative (aka risk taking) ... perhaps being "out on a limb" is an inside joke.

Thank you for having perfect communication timing for me!

Sniffily Yours ...
Roz

Sent from my iPad

From: RALPH
Sent: Saturday, January 26, 2019 at 11:10 PM
To: Roz
Subject: Best Laid Plans ...

Oh, what a bummer for you! I'm so sorry that your remaining time with Karen was cut short. However, your decision based on the knowledge of likely travel conditions tomorrow, is indicative of your sound judgment. My mother would cheer your decision. She always favored expedience when I traveled with my family between Michigan and Missouri. After my return trip to Boston last summer, driving two days through heavy rain and wind on the Interstate highways, that's absolutely to be avoided. Perhaps my incoming mail through your letter slot will take your mind off the loss of companionship. A large order for my meager efforts. I'll have to get cracking on my travel plans to PBI, and make a personal appearance at your doorstep!

Regarding those situations where a leftover part remains after you've assembled something, have you ever considered: suppose the packer in the shipping department throws one extra screw or bracket into the box, just to confound you? There are "weasels" that do such things!

Architects are either out on a limb or up on a pedestal. In both cases they usually put themselves there. Have you read "The Fountainhead"? Ah, that sad misguided Ayn Rand! Regarding architects as risk-takers, building codes are the bane of architects, and due to building inspectors, risk is reined in, not entirely but somewhat. That's an example of what Alfred North Whitehead referred to when he said, "Art flourishes where there is a sense of nothing having been done before, of complete freedom to experiment; but when caution comes in you get repetition, and repetition is the death of art."

Well, that's my lecture for your edification tonight. :-) I hope you'll rest well now, reflecting on the joyful days you spent with your family as you drift into dreamland. You'll be thinking of them ... I'll be thinking of you.

Ralph

From: Roz
Sent: Sunday, January 27, 2019 at 3:56 PM
To: RALPH
Subject: Re: Best Laid Plans ...

Thank you, Ralph, for your supportive words, sensitive expressions and understanding of my temporary need to regroup!

Weather did not disappoint confirming our correct decision to send Karen on her way yesterday ahead of storms. She is making amazing mileage progress through one state after another and will arrive at her home destination tomorrow! Just another one of her "remarkabilities"!

Happy to report that I am back to me! Being adaptable has been a mainstay for me and although momentary emotions can cloud the trees from the forest, clarity finds me quickly, and I am able to carry on! New day!

Thank you for reminding me about Ayn Rand's connection to architects as the heroic figure (embodiment of the perfect ethical and creative specimen). My late night tutorial was a bit challenging so with your permission, I will not move to the front row seat just yet ...

So relieved to know about the "weasels" and appreciate your ability to identify the unknown so confidently! Your insights never cease to amaze me!

I am eager to learn what surprises may reach my mailbox in days to come. Hoping your Sunday has been fulfilling for you in special ways!

Roz

Sent from my iPhone

• • •

From: Roz
Sent: Monday, January 28, 2019 at 5:11 PM
To: RALPH
Subject: "End of Session" ... New Chapter Begins ... (New Yorker Cartoon card) insert, maybe

Dear Ralph,
Thank you for # 4 "New Yorker" cartoon card! Cannot believe for one moment you have "features" other than interesting! You definitely misspelled this ... love pennies for thoughts ... no inflation please!

My turn to send you missives with messages ... thank heavens for Forever Stamps! Speaking of inflation ... may have to budget using email or text! By the by ... it was so nice to talk to you twice in a short span of time! I liked the casual connection that just feels so natural and comfortable ... as though you were only blocks away! Really cool ...

I am now focusing on a brief questionnaire that will ask your preferences and solicit routines that can be achieved at this B&B. Stay tuned and stay in touch!

Happy Days Ahead aka "The RI 3 Days and 4 Nights Visit/Tour"!!

Your Dedicated Guide

Sent from my iPhone

From: RALPH
Sent: Monday, January 28, 2019 at 11:37 PM
To: Roz
Subject: Re: "End of Session" … New Chapter Begins …

Dear Roz,
So, #4 arrived at your door. I hope you had a good laugh. I sort of thought that last one was the funniest … considering someone like her, spending time pondering such wealth, she'll likely be fired for not getting her work done.

Here's something for you to ponder:
Depart BOS Monday, Feb 25, 2019 @ 2:53 pm Jet Blue Flt #1921.
Arrive PBI Feb 25, 2019 @ 6:20 pm.
Depart PBI Friday, March 1, 2019 @ 6:00 am Jet Blue Flt #1022.
Arrive BOS Mar 1, 2019 @ 9:04 am.

I enjoyed the phone chats this morning because I had something to tell you to make you happy! That is if you can overlook the 6:00 am departure on March 1st!

Your questionnaire sounds like fun … lay it on me! I'm excited to see what the RLB&B will reveal. I'm confident your charm and good taste will be apparent throughout your home, and I'll be delighted. Don't go overboard preparing for me. Remember I'm just a very common guy.

Had another late night here. Spent too much time paying bills and getting tax info together. All that paperwork … my next mountain to climb. Pardon me for having you last on my list. Of course, you are the one I'm still thinking of as I close my eyes and proceed to dream.

RHI

From: Roz
Sent: Tuesday, January 29, 2019 at 12:07 PM
To: RALPH
Subject: Here We Go!

Dear RHI,
There is not a moment needed to ponder your Jet Blue itinerary! Sleep
is overrated so a "dawning departure" March 1st is doable! No worries.

In the spirit of "no moss gathers under my rock", I am emailing the first
of a sequence of easy questions that will provide the B&B Proprietress
parameters to customize your time in the land of the swaying palms to
your comfort and liking.

You may wish to Google some sites to assist in your feedback or you
can just "wing it" as risk takers/architects are prone to do (heard from
reliable source).

The topics of inquiry are not listed in order of priority since your visit
is considered a Priority!

A. Please note your Breakfast preferences. B. Please identify your
exercise regimen, if you have one (time of day and activity ... walking,
swimming, driving the car) C. Do you prefer 3 meals a day? Two? Two
and a half? D. Favorite snacks E. Favorite Dinner Adventures (French,
Italian, Thai, Fish/Seafood) for 2 of the 3 evenings ... please note the 3rd
Dinner will hopefully be a Chef Raoul Happening! F. Please rank the
following suggested activities in order of preference: Norton Museum
of Art in West Palm Beach (recently renovated to accommodate larger
exhibit inventory and public space), Elliott Museum in Stuart (vintage
car collection plus other fun collections), Flagler Museum in WPB
(historical home and collections), Morikami Museum and Japanese
Gardens in Delray Beach, beach picnic or lunch at Beach Restaurant
Juno or Riviera Beach, Worth Avenue architectural walking tour
("Rodeo Drive" on the east coast ... a mile from Mar a Lago) in PB, drive
to Miami to view city/ Miami Beach and eat famous Joe's Stone Crabs
(1.5 hour drive), movies ("Green Book" and others).

Acknowledging this is a work in progress, YOUR input, feedback,
comments, observations, objections, embellishments are vital and
welcomed. The only time-sensitive responses requested are your dinner

preferences that need reservations in this height of season challenge. Sadly, there are no Symphony, Opera or Theatre options during these dates.

I am imagining your expression … I am available to chat about any and all of these queries. I really want you to enjoy the weather and the environs and will follow your lead as you wish.

Thank you in advance for embracing my A personality with its organizing characteristics beyond beyond … Hope you are smiling in anticipation of your February plan!

Sent from my iPad

**From: RALPH
Sent: Tuesday, January 29, 2019 at 11:27 PM
To: Roz
Subject: Re: Here We Go!**

Hi Roz,
You really are organized and cover a lot of ground too. That's not a negative for me … I just wish I was so effective with getting right into the game and doing it in such orderly fashion.
As a first response, speaking of food in general, I doubt you'll have any difficulty pleasing me. I eat almost everything, and when there's something new to me (as fennel or leeks or soft-shell crab were until recently) I dig in and usually enjoy it.

Your national cuisine favorites have long been on our list too: French, Italian, Portuguese, and Thai. And the great satisfaction of moving to the east coast was the constant proximity to great seafood.

Breakfast is important to me, so it's usually hardy. Hot oatmeal with raisins or blueberries, cold cereal with berries or banana, melon, grapes, soft-boiled eggs, scrambled eggs with mushrooms, finger-size Nurnberger bratwursts, fresh French bread, croissants, plain bagels with lox and cream cheese, Jewish or Danish pastries. Of course, I don't eat all of that at the same time. It's pick and choose to assemble a good breakfast. Have I tired you out already?

Lunch is usually skipped, or light. I'll prepare a cut of French bread topped with a bit of brie or liver pâté , with a glass of milk. It's more like a snack.

Dinner menus are more elaborate ... some protein, starch, and vegetables or salad. Beef filet, pork loin, and chicken are my favorites, pasta varieties, rice (steamed or stir-fried with veggies), potatoes, any and all vegetables. A bit of "sweets" (not a lot) is a nice way to finish off.

You suggested that perhaps I should prepare a dinner one evening. I'd be happy to do that but am curious about what you abstain from. Pork? Shellfish? Dairy? What???

Snacks are quite simple: Popcorn is my favorite, but chips, almonds, Brazil nuts, all fill the bill!

My exercise is simple too. I love to walk, I'm not a good swimmer but I enjoy floating, paddling, and breast-stroking around in the water, biking, and playing catch. (Will your grandson be around) ? Indoors I do arm stretches with rubber tension straps, lifts with 5# hand weights, and body bends and twists.

Your suggestions for places to visit and activities we might partake of are appealing. I like The Norton Museum of Art, the Morikami Museum and Gardens, and the Flagler Museum. Elliott Museum may be an attraction worthy of a stop ... not for its vintage car exhibition, but for the other collections.

If the weather favors us, your idea for lunch at Juno Beach or Riviera Beach sounds novel and casual, a bright idea. I will like any opportunity we find to break for a bit of rest and quiet conversation between us. Worth Avenue doesn't resonate much like that. Miami Beach and Joe's Stone Crabs gets my attention though. What are stone crabs ... I mean, how are they prepared? I'd find that original.

Now that the trip is planned, I'm elated and shortly will be chomping at the bit to get going. We are flexible, so if we don't get to cover all the significant landmarks this trip, we'll do it later. What I'm hoping for is calm balmy weather and time for us to quietly talk indoors and out, to reach a better understanding about who we are.

As you hoped, I'm smiling!
Count Raoul ... Chef Raoul and everything in between

From: Roz
Sent: Friday, February 1, 2019 at 10:01 AM
To: RALPH
Subject: Thursday Night Happening!

Hi Ralph,
This is where and what I was about last night. I look forward to sharing this experience with you during one of our "getting to know you" chats in this month of February!

Hope the frigid temps are quickly rising and that you will be out and about with less layers very soon! Although the huge rise in temp numbers is predicted for Boston, I can guarantee balmy temps for you during your R&R sojourn.

Take care!
Roz

From: RALPH
Sent: Friday, February 1, 2019 at 10:19 PM
To: Roz
Subject: Re: Thursday Night Happening!

Dear Roz,
You informed me that the forthcoming temp numbers for Boston will be rising. That is a fact. Each day we've experienced gradual rising, and this coming Monday 56 degrees F is predicted. Oh well, even if it should remain that high here-on-out, I'm still dedicated to getting with you in the balmy, palmy, Sunshine state!

Your email arrived while I was preparing for my day away from home. When I caught sight of your name in my inbox, I went right to it. The attachment caught my interest, and I wanted to respond immediately … but uh uh! Regrettably it was time for me to get going to Brookline. My day for daycare of my youngest granddaughter was today, and I was already a bit late. So, I departed, but was thinking most of the day about getting back to you. So here I am, but probably too late for you to get this yet today. So, let's consider it a Saturday morning greeting.

Happy February. It won't take so long for me to arrive this month … February has only 28 days

Pardon me now as I slip into my white smock and get back to my cleaning!

Ralph

• • •

From: Roz
Sent: Tuesday, February 5, 2019 at 5:04 PM
To: RALPH
Subject: Recycling

Hi Ralph,
Thinking of you and wanted to share this moment with you. Snapped this picture of a Blue Heron sunning itself on this picture perfect day at the Oceanographic Museum in Stuart, Florida today. This was the excursion today for The Culture Club (once a month happening with a group of women interested in "growing ourselves" through cultural and educational experiences). Over the years this eclectic group has had many laughs in a variety of venues! Lots of stories to share! Last month toured The Sanitation Facility! Learned about how important recycling is and how garbage converted to electricity saves much for us Florida Power Light customers!

Hope you have had a lovely warm day!

BTW ... yesterday's morning phone chat was fun! Great way to start the day ...

From: RALPH
Sent: Tuesday, February 5, 2019 at 10:00 PM
To: Roz
Subject: Re: Recycling

A few years ago, I saw a report on recycling trash in a Japanese city. The photos accompanying were amazing. The building was expansive and very glassy so the public could see the processing throughout. The personnel doing the work wore white uniforms, with white caps and boots, and white gloves. And they were all clean! Clearly the attitude was order, cleanliness, pride ... it was not considered demeaning or beneath one's dignity to do that work. There's an interesting psychology at work there.

Your Culture Club is rather impressive ... one of the "lights" of Florida.

The phone call yesterday was a great way to start the day. I should be so imaginative! Will be back atcha soon.

Ralph

• • •

From: RALPH
Date: Wednesday, February 6, 2019 at 1:49 PM
To: Roz
Subject: Blue Heron

Hi Roz,
A happy hello to you. I was up early this morning, slipped into some clothes and went to work on my taxes. Then decided I better have some breakfast. A little of this and a bit of that ... and here I am at noon finally getting to you. I must begin getting my priorities straight!

Your trip to the Oceanic Museum sounds fascinating. That's a lot of water-life to check out. You were kind thinking of me and sending the heron photo. It's a bird of which I have some familiarity. In Michigan our home had a view across a marsh off a small lake nearby. Blue herons frequently landed there and motionless would wait to strike minnows or small frogs. Having their fill, they would take off, beautiful in their graceful ascent aloft.

Our weather here can certainly accommodate a trip or two out into the natural environment. The air is wonderful. Yesterday I had to go out for a medical appointment and to pick up some shirts from the cleaners. I headed out to the garage, then halfway there turned around and came back in to put on a light jacket. Gonna be a real bummer when the normal weather comes back for the next couple months.

Your trip must have exposed you to a lot of ocean science, though I imagine you have visited there before. The oceans are so vast, and my knowledge about them is so vapid. My misfortune ... to be such a landlubber! Was it my fate that my origin was in small-town Missouri? I should have made acquaintance with you back then.

You told me of your "eclectic group" having many laughs, and you made me laugh when you mentioned a previous trip to the Sanitation facility. I was glad to read that it was the recycling center, not the sewage treatment center!

Ralph

• • •

From: Roz
Sent: Sunday, February 10, 2019 at 5:07 PM
To: RALPH
Subject: Today was Special!

Dear Ralph,
Thanks to our warm, wonderful conversation this morning (with the exception of your "mishap"), I was primed for the Russian National Orchestra's emotionally thrilling all Rachmaninoff performance at 2pm (the third of my Symphony Series of 4).

The first half of the program had me in deep sighs and tears with two of my favorites ... "Vocalise" and "Piano Concerto No 2" in C minor, Op 18. You were in my thoughts as I experienced the breathless beauty of the music "beyond beyond" ... as was the incredible pianist George Li (American pianist and recent graduate of the Harvard/New England Conservatory joint program).

Hope your Sunday was a smiling one for you, too!
Me

Sent from my iPhone

From: RALPH
Sent: Sunday, February 10, 2019 at 11:04 PM
To: Roz
Subject: Re: Today was Special!

Dear "Me",
Oh, dear me indeed! Does anyone ever tire of hearing Rachmaninoff's Piano Concerto No. 2 in C minor? How I wish I'd been there to share the moment with you. You are blessed to have such outstanding musicians

coming there and stirring your emotions. The other composition, Vocalise, is not familiar to me so I googled it and found a performance featuring Joshua Bell. Such power in the violin, grabbing at your heart! What an engaging afternoon for you.

Interesting to hear that the pianist is out of the Harvard/NE Conservatory program. (After my wife and I moved to Boston, we started contributing to the NEC and attended their performances almost weekly.) Now about the pianist you heard today, it caught my attention because our little church has a new pianist. Our former pianist moved away, and this young man who had begun attending services volunteered. For a couple months now I've gotten to know him, having given him rides from church to the Longy School, to save him the nuisance of bus transport during this bitter cold season. He's a fine young man and an accomplished musician.

Its gotten late. I have to hit the sack. I wanted to respond to you earlier, but I failed. Maybe you'll enjoy finding it in the morning. Think of me smiling!

Me Too

• • •

From: RALPH
Sent: Tuesday, February 12, 2019 at 6:22 PM
To: Roz
Subject: Will you recognize me when I arrive?

Hi Roz,
Talking with you was a nice interlude ... it gave me a bit of a boost, to disregard the blowing snow outside. While I'm doing my best to stay warm, you're probably trying to cool off!

Mori sent me a few family pics recently, some taken when I stayed for dinner with them after an afternoon with my granddaughter. One of the images was rather charming as I performed some of my artistry, coloring her fingernails as well as pleasing her. The thought occurred to me ... is that the fellow Roz remembers? Then I couldn't resist sending you the picture taken as I picked up my other granddaughter after school wearing my brown Fedora.

The third pic (black-and-white) I'm sending to add some mirth to the mix. I found it in the back of a drawer when I was into house-cleaning a couple weeks ago. It was "snapped" about a month after I returned home from my military service in Germany ... the hair on top had grown out, but the sides were slow in doing their part.

Don't take any of these to your framer!
Ralph

• • •

The sight of you
Is so much like
Sunshine.
I'm wondering...
Will you be my
Valentine?

Thinking about
you and smiling!

R

From: RALPH
Sent: Thursday, February 14, 2019 at 4:36 PM
To: Roz
Subject: Valentine's Day

Dear, dear, Roz,
Your card delighted me. I wish I had come up with one so kinetic and innovative. You are expected to have live flamingos welcoming me on arrival. That was such a clever flamingoing means of aptly closing the visual, while subtly revealing a Valentine heart. The question remaining in my mind is, was that Roz Flamingo or Ralph Flamingo that chose to move with the crowd...but realized quickly that a "groupie" seldom enjoys the "whoopee"! I'm dreaming now of walking the beach with you...both of us in pink!

You're precious!

Pushing days out of my way, excited to see you.
Ralph

• • •

From: Roz
Sent: Saturday, February 16, 2019 at 9:56 PM
To: RALPH
Subject: Thank you!

Dear Ralph,
I am so grateful and so relieved that we are able to talk easily and honestly about so many things. The depth of feeling and heartfelt sharing is very important to me.

Thank you for letting me feel safe and comfortable in our communication.

Sweet dreams.

Sent from my iPhone

From: RALPH
Sent: Saturday, February 16, 2019 at 11:57 PM
To: Roz
Subject: Re: Thank you!

Roz

It was a good discussion we had this afternoon, about some issues that aren't just superficial ... they are embedded in our upbringing. I'm pleased that you are comfortable opening up such topics, prepared to clear the air. If we should happen to come up with something about which we are on opposite sides, I believe we can bridge that gap. I say that because I'm friends with too many Republicans with whom I disagree, but I value some of their other interests.

I was somewhat shocked after getting off the phone with you because I believe we talked for almost an hour and a half. So, you see, that's how meaningful conversation with you is. I will find it so much more significant when I can sit near you soon, to watch as you speak, and from my own face you'll recognize my excitement, agreement, humor or my desire to break in and respond to you.

It seems prescient that I didn't wait until evening to call you, or you may not have heard from me. I wanted to prepare some food for our church lunch tomorrow (some persons like to contribute a favorite dish that they do well) so I considered putting you "on the back burner" and doing the preparation before calling you. But I reversed and called you first. I finally got around to my cooking about 7 p.m. and was at it until 10. And then the clean-up after. Coming up to my office I found your sweet email and couldn't let that sit without responding. So here I am.

You're no doubt wondering just what I'm taking to the church event. Well, it's a big pot of corn chowder and French bread to go with it. I've made it before, but I sure don't remember having to prepare so much chopped celery, onions, potatoes, corn, and the special ingredient fried bacon bits. My kitchen, after all, could challenge an Army mess hall, but the chowder is superb!

Well, enough! This was a day of cooking, and I thank the Lord for my dishwasher. Hoping you're sleeping soundly, which I'll be doing just minutes from now.

Have a great Sunday. I hope it's dry.
Soupy Sales

From: Roz
Sent: Monday, February 18, 2019 at 10:22 AM
To: RALPH
Subject: Saving my southern belle accent for "in person" for "in waiting"

Simply cannot fathom how you manage to push the clever/charm button up a notch will each email missive!!! Boggles this mind … requires reality check in a week!

About "reality" now that you have reached the "closet/drawer dynamic" … please note "casual" is the state of affairs (pack no tie or jacket) … daytime temps will be in the high 70's with rain forecast percentage as intermittent … may touch 80ish. Evenings may drop into low 70's … may touch high 60's as the coolest. Please be prepared for 24/7 air conditioning as you will be in a tropical setting (no natives) … will require a reset for your frame of reference for February.

I know you know all of this … just needed an excuse to email so I can be the recipient of your happily anticipated response!

Happy Monday!
Sent from my iPhone

From: RALPH
Sent: Monday, February 18, 2019 at 4:18 PM
To: Roz
Subject: Re: Saving my southern belle accent for "in person" or "in waiting"

OK … the doctor is in!

Waking this morning, the muted sound of the Parkway traffic led me to believe it had snowed overnight. So, I looked, and it had! A lovely 3 or 4 inch layer blanketed the area. It was 5:30 a.m. so there was almost no evidence in the snow of human life on the move around here (that is if you're able to blot the Parkway from memory). I got up for a quick trip to the bathroom, then slipped back to bed. I had my second awakening at 7:15, decided it would be a good idea to rise and get myself going.

After showering et al, I went down for some breakfast to fortify myself, then bundled up and went out to face the snow!

My neighbor has always offered me use of his snowblower, so I headed for his garage. Always do his driveway first, then proceed to do mine. By the time I cleared all of it and came inside it was nearly 2 p.m. Late last Friday I found a message on my phone from my cardiologist, to make an appointment for an echo, so I thought I better get that taken care of before I forget and travel south.

By the way, since we're celebrating Washington's Birthday, I'm not lying to you today!

Did love finding your message and I respect the guidelines you set. The temps you noted sound wonnnnnderful. It doesn't sound half bad there on the "back burner". Yuh give me feeeever!

Happy Monday? Yes, I've just been writing to the best part of my Monday. One week now ... can't wait! As for this moment, I want your smile meter to go way beyond SUPERB.
Your faithful boggler

· · ·

From: Roz
Sent: Tuesday, February 19, 2019 at 6:43 AM
To: RALPH
Subject: This morning's view of the Full Moon and the orchid on the tree ... 2/19/2019 at 6:16am

From: RALPH
Sent: Tuesday, February 19, 2019 at 7:54 AM
To: Roz
Subject: Re: This morning's view of the Full Moon and the orchid on the tree ... 2/19/2019 at 6:16am

You've witnessed the extreme beauty of the morning, nature's gift to anyone willing to rise and explore the early hour. The hazy images of the moon views are dreamy ... really photo art. And the elegance of the orchid flower leaves me almost breathless, so sensual, the image stirs me physically. I'm grateful for the response you bring up in me.

・ ・ ・

From: Roz
Sent: Tuesday, February 19, 2019 at 2:42 PM
To: RALPH
Subject: In ANTICIPATION

OK ... Tour Guide is in!

Driving to do errands this morning, noted hibiscus in bloom (pinks and oranges), red begonias generously filling flower beds, raspberry and purple bougainvillea draping surfaces and blooming on small trees, delicate unknown small blue and white flowers in low bushes lining streets with other orange flowered hedges. Adding to the color palette are the variety of herons and egrets that walk about easily reminding us humans to "pay attention to the beauty that surrounds us" ... variety of very tall and short palm trees (recently defrocked of coconuts for safety reasons), intricately woven trunks and branches of Banyan trees and tall non-blooming (early summer brilliant flowers) graceful poinciana trees ... visual feasts await your arrival in 5 days.

Updated weather forecast suggests less rainy moments during daylight hours (yay!!) with temps unseasonably warmer than usual.

Kitchen staff has reported that breakfast and snack requests have been addressed with plenty of opportunities to indulge in spontaneous options.

Hope this update will please you as your visit will certainly be the HIGHLIGHT of the B&B's Season and Beyond!

Enthusiastically Yours,
Your Tour Guide ... Your One and Only Personal Guide for This Sojourn

From: RALPH
Sent: Tuesday, February 19, 2019 at 5:21 PM
To: Roz
Subject: Re: In ANTICIPATION

Now my feet are restless!

It's apparent the Tour Guide had her eyes wide open when she was out!

That's a marvelous collection of nature's finest, seeming to be an ideal route for walking. It's great to have the early revival of flowering plants. Up here we have to wait so long for the blossoms and colors to return to the scene. Years ago we had a potted hibiscus which we put out in May and brought inside in September. The blossoms were beautiful. I think we gave it to a friend when we moved. I'm curious about poinciana trees, which I don't believe I've ever seen anywhere. Do you have mango trees around you?

Mori visited a Florida girl a couple times down there, and her parents had a mango tree. He'd bring back mangoes for me. After my arrival you better be ready for lots of questions.

The weather report is positive … while I know I'll enjoy your home; it will be excellent if we can get some good hours outdoors too. Even so, from what you've told me, it doesn't rain all day!

Roz, I don't want you to stock up with lots of edibles for my pleasure. You are so gracious, and I know you'll want to provide everything I like, but I don't want you left with the remains when I'm gone. I'm sure we'll be dining well with any of the food items you have in your pantry. Sharing the table with you will be most important, the ultimate pleasure.

Your update not only pleases me, it assures me that you are as excited about the things we'll do together as I am. I'm betting that my "Enthusiastically" overwhelms your "Enthusiastically"!

BP … normal

From: Roz
Sent: Tuesday, February 19, 2019 at 10:56 PM
To: RALPH
Subject: A Horticulturist I am Not …

Normally I would say "bring it on" referring to questions … please keep in mind that I appreciate the beauty of nature as an observer for the most part. Not sure I will be knowledgeable re: origin of species , best growing cycle and recommended fertilizer … do know there can be a fungus among us and nasty bugs that relish eating innocent beauties … but, I will do my best and when in doubt refer you to Google!

Glad to know you have "happy feet" since there is much to see and do depending on the time and place and preference. Fun times await you with songs to sing ... No worries about foodstuffs and quantity ... lucky for me, I like much of your routine nourishment.

Signing off with happy thoughts knowing your BP is normal!

Enthusiastically Plus

Sent from my iPad

From: RALPH
Sent: Wednesday, February 20, 2019 at 9:10 AM
To: Roz
Subject: Re: A Horticulturist I am Not ...

My expectation is of an amazing collection of flora there, growing in abundance as natural habitat, while my knowledge of those species, from where I come, is we have them only propagated and nurtured to be admired and enjoyed. I envy you for what you have so commonly in view. But I won't burden you with "interrogation overload".

I have happy feet and a happy face, just from anticipation of the coming week. Despite 17 degrees F we have bright sunshine today, and that's the spirit with which I'll arrive. And by the way, you're a Plus far beyond enthusiasm!

Flying Tiger ... arriving soon

* * *

From: Roz
Sent: Wednesday, February 20, 2019 at 10:15 PM
To: RALPH
Subject: Don't want to sound like "a recording" ...

But ... heard the weather forecast for your neck of the leafless woods (unless you have pines/evergreens in your "woods") that white stuff is falling and may accumulate ... then some other precipitation as temps rise?? Thinking about you bundled in the elements 'doing your thing". Sorry you need to snow blow and shovel yet again so soon.

Just thinking about you and wishing you were here this week to miss this wintry moment.

Take care.

From: RALPH
Sent: Wednesday, February 20, 2019 at 11:01 PM
To: Roz
Subject: Re: Don't want to sound like "a recording" …

Hi,
You caught me just in time. I was preparing to put this machine to "sleep" when I found your email. You are correct, light snow is falling now. It's doubtful much will accumulate because the temperature is expected to rise later and the precip will change to rain. The report says that will wash much of the snow away. I'm planning to lie low tomorrow. There will have to be five or six inches for me to go out there and blow it away.

I checked the West Palm Beach weather and found that you're having quite a nice week … in the 80's. But it looks like rain is in our future, 40% and 60% during the middle three days of my visit. Too bad I couldn't get on an earlier flight Monday. Things are looking pretty nice for that day. Well, we're troupers that can handle it! Though if the rain persists, I'd prefer we were groupers! If you're still up let me wish you sound sleep and a good night. If you're already breathing zzzzzzzzzzzzz's, then you'll have this to wake up to.

Sandman

• • •

From: Roz
Sent: Thursday, February 28, 2019 at 08:26 AM
To: RALPH
Subject: Breakfast view "The Garden of Eden"
Attachments: IMG_4183.jpg

IMG_4183.jpg

From: RALPH
Sent: Friday, March 1, 2019 at 8:27 AM
To: Roz
Subject: Re: Breakfast view "The Garden of Eden"

Hi Presch,
Everything smooth thru security, brief wait at gate, then boarded. On-time departure on a larger plane. Flight time to Boston 2 hrs. 30 min.) Had "breakfast" ... coffee from Jet Blue and bless you for that wonderful scone. That will hold me until I am home.

We're high above a cloudscape and the sunshine puts me back in touch with you. The glow of your face and the sparkle in your eyes comes to mind again. The "first thing" chats with you each morning were truly a relaxing way to commence the day. I'm certain I'll reflect on those moments in the days ahead.

Let me tell you again how wonderful the four days we shared were. By your warmth and grace, I'm confident you feel the same.

Love to you,
Ralph

From: Roz
Sent: Friday, March 1, 2019 at 09:06 AM
To: RALPH
Subject: Re:Breakfast view "The Garden Eden"

Dearest Stud muffin,
Does this email indicate you have landed safely? I am loving your missive once again!

Huggiest Hugs,
Sparkle Plenty

PS ... off to fund raise now!

Sent from my iPhone

• • •

From: RALPH
Sent: Saturday, March 2, 2019 at 2:55 PM
To: Roz
Subject: This and That

Hey ... how's your dey? You don't sey!

Roz you were right. We're having snow. It's very powdery, and I feel good being inside. It may end by evening, at which time I'll go out and do some clearing of the driveway, so I can get out tomorrow for the Sabbath service. Just looking out now, it appears to be less than 3 inches. Having just come from PBG, any snow at all wins my Ugh Award!

When I got up this morning it was still clear outside. I thought it prudent to get to the market before the mess started, so before breakfast I went out for the necessities I needed. Nevertheless, the snow arrived before I got going. Traffic was very light, which was an advantage. Also, the market was not a tangle of people.

I think somewhere in your impressive B&B you have a guest umbrella. When I unpacked, my little black one was absent. It may be somewhere in the bedroom I used, like under the edge of the bed. Or maybe in the sunroom, where I may have put it on the table while waiting for us to go out. Maybe I kicked it under my car seat, or it's on the back seat floor, or in the trunk. Well, don't be concerned about it, it's not important enough. If you find it, use it!

Something I didn't forget or lose is this innovative travel cup. It's sitting here by me (and I regret the giver isn't across from me). The cup is so well designed, great for taking hot or cold drinks on a drive and keeping me always mindful of you. You look so good in pink! As for me, I'm practicing standing on one leg. Observant bystanders will be envious that I've been to Florida!

Now I'm cutting you off ... to avoid endangering myself with carpal tunnel damage. How's that for an eqskewss? Oh-oh, brain cells are already breaking down! I'm stopping now because I have more things to wash.

Meanwhile, stay here in my heart.

Lord of the laundry

From: RALPH
Sent: Sunday, March 3, 2019 at 9:06 AM
To: Roz
Subject: It's a beautiful day in the neighborhood

Came down a few minutes ago to begin breakfast, but only after first starting Bach's 2nd Piano Concerto. It is ethereal! Plus, it brings me closer to you. Immerse yourself in music this afternoon. 143 all over again!

Yours

· · ·

From: Roz
Sent: Sunday, March 3, 2019 at 5:13 PM
To: RALPH
Subject: My Afternoon with Itzak

If facial expressions could talk, Itzak Perlman would convey every emotion known to humankind. His virtuosity is extraordinary, but his face tells it All! After ovation after ovation, Itzak rode his scooter back on the stage and played six additional pieces (including John Williams' "Schindler's List") prefaced with his humorous intros and joy of the moment. Wish you could have shared this with me!

From: RALPH
Sent: Sunday, March 3, 2019 at 10:16 PM
To: Roz
Subject: Re: My Afternoon with Itzak

You're reading me perfectly ... I would have loved sharing the program with you. And wow, a six composition encore. That's almost like a double program. He's a great violinist despite his handicap. The man always seems so happy too, when so many of us whimper and complain over the simplest of concerns. (Forgive me, Lord!)

Last night I was late to bed, so this early afternoon I napped for about an hour. Felt great getting up. Ran out to pick up a few items, then prepared dinner. Watched a bit of news ... old stuff about Trump so I flipped it off and decided to get into writing a note to Steve. With the weather forecast for tomorrow I'm beginning to wonder if my mail will be delivered and collected. I'm sure you've been watching and heard about the main load of snow dropping on the Boston area, giving us maybe 10 inches by commuter peak travel time.

My BP has been very good since I'm home, every day below 120/80. Heart rate too, in the 80's. I have a medical appointment scheduled for 10:30 a.m., but that may change when we see how much snow we have early morning. Of course, I could hitch a ride on the snowplow!

I notice it's after 10 p.m. already so I think I'll close down for the night. Sorry I've been cut out of great music and warm temps now. But I wish the best for you … great days back with "the women's club".

Miss you!

. . .

From: Roz
Sent: Tuesday, March 5, 2019 at 8:17 PM
To: RALPH
Subject: Hmmm … your turn or my turn?

From: RALPH
Sent: Tuesday, March 5, 2019 at 11:03 PM
To: Roz
Subject: Re: Hmmm … your turn or my turn?

Dear Flaminga,
That item floating in front of them isn't familiar, but if they are expecting to get in, they better be able to retract those legs or fold them tightly!

Best to you,
Flamingo
PS - You'll notice, of course, the gender reference. The feminine suffix is "inga" whereas the masculine is "ingo".

. . .

From: Roz
Sent: Wednesday, March 6, 2019 at 9:47 PM
To: RALPH
Subject: Wednesday Night Intellectual Pursuits- Bible Study Ibsen-Hnath Study

From: RALPH
Sent: Wednesday, March 06, 2019 at 11:35 PM
To: Roz
Subject: Re: Wednesday Night Intellectual Pursuits- Bible Study Ibsen-Hnath Study

Thanks for forwarding that copy about the play and playwright. I haven't been able to get into it tonight but will tomorrow. Then if we talk about it, I'll be better prepared to exchange thoughts with you.

I got home about 9:00 p.m., having had a little chat with Calvin after the study period. Then I settled down to write a letter response to my cousin in Arizona. She wrote me over a month ago and I just kept putting the letter off. Now it's taken care of. So, I'm tired and ready to sink into the mattress for about seven hours. BTW, what was the name of that mattress on the bed where I slept?

Oh, one more thing. Thanks for the picture you sent. You look so impressive, with your hair looking comfortably casual, but under control. It reminds me of those fashion mag pics with the woman strolling the avenue, hair flowing with the breeze. Cool mama, I like it. I'll try to talk with you tomorrow.

Luffin-muffin

• • •

From: RALPH
Sent: Thursday, March 7, 2019 at 3:50 PM
To: Roz
Subject: Re: For Your Collection

Wow, you look so lovely and graceful in both pictures. I think we did so many pix either from waist upward or seated that I didn't consider how shapely and poised you truly are. I've told you how impressed I am by your height, so tall and majestic as you are. It would be a proud moment to see you coming up the red carpet. They are wonderful pictures, and thanks for entrusting them to me.

From: RALPH
Sent: Thursday, March 7, 2019 at 3:53 PM
To: Roz
Subject: Re: For Your Collection

This picture in the front garden is so inviting ... great to be out hand in hand during a leisurely stroll. What a great time it would be!

From: RALPH
Sent: Friday, March 8, 2019 at 7:23 AM
To: Roz
Subject: Re: For Your Collection

I've just finished my morning bathroom ritual, all the while listening to Music Choice "Soundscapes". The one segment is "My Orchid Spirit" and it reminds me of you. I hope your day is bright and enthralling.

· · ·

From: Roz
Sent: Friday, March 8, 2019 at 7:46 AM
To: RALPH
Subject: Pre-Dawn a week ago!

Dear Squeaky Clean,
I am SMILING as I snuggle amid the sheets thinking about you a week ago as we departed for the airport for your very, very early return to Boston ... fast forward to lasting influences we left upon each other (Soundscapes for You and Heartscapes for me)!

Wishing you a lovely day with your granddaughter.

Presch (my new fav),
Roz

Sent from my iPad

Don't get on . . .

. . . Lest you seal
your fate.
Hell is not
FLAMING,
It's FREEZING!

Alas, you learned
too late!

(♥ You warned me)

From: RALPH
Sent: Friday, March 8, 2019 at 8:46 AM
To: Roz
Subject: Re: Pre-Dawn a week ago!

Hi Presch,
After reading your salutation, I'm SMILING more. I am squeaky, but I think it's coming from my joints! You're right ... we did exchange influences during our time together, and now the music keeps me in touch with you despite the distance between us.

The sun is shining, BP is normal, and you've written. Life is great!

Mr. Clean

• • •

From: Roz
Sent: Saturday, March 9, 2019 at 7:25 PM
To: RALPH
Subject: Hello Robin on a snowy branch ...

Dear Creative One,
Now that I am cuckoo from taxation, I can easily communicate with the Cardinal looking at a very inviting door of a snow covered house in a very northern clime ... lucky for us no fate has been sealed, despite poetics!

Happy to have signed phase one of tax document completion ... time for chocolate!!

Sweets to you, hoping you will entertain another boarding pass in the not too distant future.

Chirpingly Yours.

Sent from my iPhone

From: RALPH
Sent: Saturday, March 9, 2019 at 10:35 PM
To: Roz
Subject: Re: Hello Robin on a snowy branch ...

Hi Presch,
Happy to know my greeting made it to your door today... not withholding it from you two more days. That dear chirping cardinal is the one good thing that prevailed after the snowstorm, although all around that early morning it was virginal.

I'm happy too that you've survived Phase 1 of "tax hell", plus I love your choice of reward. I better send you some to replenish your supply.

Yours truly is in sync with you about boarding passes ... or in lieu of Jet Bleu maybe go prospecting for a Delorean to rocket me back to "your future". Choosing how and when is on my mind. (Ah, yes, a rocket to zap me back to you ... do you happen to have Elon Musk's phone number for me)?

Disregard all this nonsense and think positively. It will happen. For Lent I have to give something up ... I've decided it will be one hour of sleep tonight!

Smarty Pants

· · ·

From: Roz
Sent: Monday, March 11, 2019 at 9:36 AM
To: RALPH
Subject: Springing Forward

Good morning,
Hope you are refreshed after "catchup sleep" ... I felt the same loss of the one hour yesterday and went to bed early feeling extra tired ... funny how sensitive our biorhythms can be to a one hour adjustment when we are in our "at home dynamic" compared to how our biorhythms adjust when we are traveling in foreign countries many hours ahead of our normal timing. Must be the mind body connection that pushes our circadian rhythm to embrace the time change in exciting surroundings.

Yesterday was "keep friend company" day not cultural enrichment day for me. Since my Symphony Series has ended for this season, I will experience "Culture" on a variety of days (tomorrow I will view the "Culture Club" experience as we tour the Bush exhibit "Portraits of Courage: A Commander in Chiefs Tribute to American Warriors" at The Society of the Four Arts) and will share thoughts with you if you wish. I spent yesterday afternoon "keeping company" with a special friend of some 40 years who had a dermatology treatment on her face for possible skin cancer that requires no sunlight for 3 days. I was day 3 company and diversion ... she is lovely, and we have a wonderful friendship history ... both she and her husband were so supportive during my early grieving stages, and I know I was important for her when her husband died four years ago. I spent times staying with her during recent summers in Maine at their beautiful cottage on the Lake.

I have been thinking ... could be dangerous, this is true ... and want to talk to you about this recent "thinking" when next we chat. No worries this is fun thinking ...

Just checked weather for you and looks like improving conditions are on your doorstep with rising temps (at last!!) and no precipitation in the forecast!

Enjoy the slight suggestion of Spring as you begin your busy and productive week! I am off to post my tax info to the accountant! Hooray!

With happy thoughts,
Presch

Sent from my iPad

From: RALPH
Sent: Monday, March 11, 2019 at 6:59 PM
To: Roz
Subject: Re: Springing Forward

Hi Presch,
You greeted me with "Good morning" and here it's already time for "Good evening". I was out of here early today going after my Monday morning list of places to go and things to get. When I was with you it

seemed like you could get out and find all the things you needed in one concentrated area of shops or services. My problem is I have to go to neighboring communities for some and wrap up in scattered locations of Cambridge. Now that I've explained it for you, I see why my gas tank is always near empty!

Such a nice letter you wrote. It's satisfying to know you have a deeply connected friendship with someone with whom you always feel comfortable and can confide in when necessary. I think it has a very solid foundation, in that you and your husband, and your friend and her husband were so bonded together. I also think such a relationship of couples is quite rare. The two of you are fortunate to have each other as you carry on, and to share such trust between you. Sorry to hear about her facial skin problem. It's a concern that I have too, having had periodic treatment on my forehead and nose. In fact, I have an appointment with my dermatologist this coming Wednesday to have a check-up.

Yes, I would like for you to share your thoughts with me, to tell me more about viewing the Bush exhibit at The Society of the Four Arts. And which Four Arts does the Society embrace?

Delighted to hear that you are scratching taxes from your list of things to do! My news for you is I received my tax forms back today and am happy to find that I owe nothing. I overpaid my estimated taxes.

So, you are "thinking", which makes me think, "what should I think she is thinking about?" It takes me back to the school picnic out at the lake. The sweet young thing says to her boyfriend, "Listen to Professor Jones, always so erudite, there in the water swimming and shouting, 'I'm thinking, I'm thinking.'" The boy replied, "You dummy, you know Professor Jones has a lisp!" Now, back to you ... tell me what you're thinking!

I'll close by thanking you for using your letter to build my vocabulary. I now know something about circadian rhythms. Ah Roz, ever the teacher. I'll bring you an apple any time. Have a good eve.

Love, Adam

. . .

From: Roz
Sent: Monday, March 11, 2019 at 10:20 PM
To: RALPH
Subject: Winding down the day with you ...

Loved reading your "letter response" to me about your Monday up and out "to do" list ... your anecdotal tidbits and keen observations always fascinate me ... I feel like a student anxious to absorb your thoughts.

Just when a thought is seriously being brewed in observation or assessment of an interesting something, up pops your humor and bingo ... a new thought enters, and we are off in another interesting direction! Reading You is the best fun!

Curious that you see the teacher in my messages (although I would welcome an apple from you often) ... that is certainly not my intent!!!

On the other hand, learning from one another is a gift to cherish and that is how I feel about your communications.

Needless to say, today's Book Club discussion can only be conveyed through conversation ... writing about the discussion will be detrimental to this screen ...

I look forward to sharing the Bush Exhibit tomorrow with you and will inquire about which of the Four Arts the Society embraces.

Pleasant dreams.
"Eve"

From: RALPH
Sent: Tuesday, March 12, 2019 at 10:43 AM
To: Roz
Subject: Re: Winding down the day with you ...

The timeline on your email from last night informed me that you were up and thinking of me. It's heartwarming to know that, and I regret I was already streaming zzzzzzzzzzzzzzzzzz's by then. But it was a delight to find your comments first thing today.

I agree with you about our communications ... it's about learning from one another. Very little from you that's mundane. You explore a lot of material, and you share it. I admire that.

As you stated, we exchange interesting observations and suddenly something humorous works its way in. I have to say you can't imagine how often I am struck by a statement or phrase in your message and burst into laughing out loud. It's such a pleasure to recognize at times your amusing take on life.

For instance, your mention of the Book Club, that "writing about the discussion will be detrimental to this screen." What immediately comes to my mind is the graphic image one often sees, of a small dot in the middle of the screen that begins to smoke and then fire spreads radially outward, destroying the entire panel. Apparently, I shall have to wait until we are side by side, to hear about the Punjabi widows' passionate experiences! (I can hear you now ... "No thank YEW")! Now that you have me fired up, I better close and get back into a cold shower. Just kidding!

Have a great day. My regrets that I'm not there to share it with you. Now I'm not kidding!

Polar Survivor

From: Roz
Sent: Tuesday, March 12, 2019 at 9:00 PM
To: RALPH
Subject: Thank YOU!

Just an FYI ... I have not stopped smiling since 6:07 pm when we hung up the phones after a heart blending conversation that spoke "bundts to nuts", every pun intended! Awash in FEELINGS that are beyond beyond just cause ...

Realized that I forgot to mention Bush's Portraits which says it all ... to me, his motivation to help Warriors exceeds his artistic talent ... he is to be admired for finding an "artistic" voice (after two years of studying painting) that helps and encourages brave service people who sacrificed hugely for our country and are deserving of the public's support and thanks!

There is NO question that sitting close to you is so-0 much better than being "bronzed"!

Utterly Yours

Sent from my iPhone

From: RALPH
Sent: Tuesday, March 12, 2019 at 10:04 PM
To: Roz
Subject: Re: Thank YOU!

Dear One,
If I stay in the sun long enough next time I'm there, I'll be able to offer you "bronzed" too, but our FEELINGS are more than skin deep!

Dear Too

. . .

From: RALPH
Sent: Wednesday, March 13, 2019 at 3:30 PM
To: Roz
Subject: My doctor appointment

Skin update:
3-13-2019   10:45 a.m.

Total body review (ummmm)
6 Liquid Nitrogen applications
1 slice from spot on scalp for biopsy
Biopsy report to follow

Dr's comment: "Ralph, you're good to go for another 100,000 miles!"

From: Roz
Sent: Wednesday, March 13, 2019 at 4:44 PM
To: RALPH
Subject: Re: My doctor appointment

Dear Dear Too,
Been thinking about your appt today and am pleased to read your report ("ummm" and all)! Nitrogen blasts seem to be the commonplace happening for us aging folks ... red spots do fade quickly after a sensitive cycle and then we feel restored to near perfection until the next visit!

Ooh, an ouchie slice for biopsy just to be sure ... wow, 100,000 miles!!! Hopefully Florida bound! Smiling ...

Now a question for Chef Raoul ... have you used a Foley Food Mill? I would like to make applesauce, and someone suggested I purchase a Foley. Your thoughts please ...

Have I mentioned that I love, love reading you or talking to you each day ... a habit I am not one bit shy about embracing!

Dear One

Sent from my iPhone

From: RALPH
Sent: Wednesday, March 13, 2019 at 11:37 PM
To: Roz
Subject: Re: My doctor appointment

Hi Dear One, at this late moment in the day, Oh my ... you wrote way back at 4:44 pm today. I was out selecting paint colors about that time. When I returned home, before I could check email or phone messages, my good friend from southern Missouri rang me up. His wife is away today, and I think he was getting lonely and decided to chat with me, which he did for almost an hour. My plan was to attend a Bible study tonight at the church, so I quickly consumed a sandwich for "dinner" and headed back to church.

Yeah, I like your suggestion of using some of those 100,000 miles to get Florida bound. I'll have to remain out of the sun, but I can sacrifice that to be near you.

Now here is where you will observe Chef Raoul clinging to his commonplace roots. I have not used a Foley Food Mill, nor have I seen one! Mori gave me a Cuisinart processor last year which I have not yet used. If it were up to me to make applesauce, I would probably steam some peeled and sliced apples, and when they are mushy, I would mash them through a sieve, sugar & spice them, and put them into the fridge ready to use. A lot less "machinery" to soak, scrub, and store out of the way.

You have told me you like what I write, and you prefer talking together likewise. I appreciate your receptivity to my things in print or in voice. But I'll tell you forthrightly that I believe I'm the lucky one, because I get to hear your lovely voice, and I delight in it! You're quite exceptional, and I pause now and then to picture you speaking in front of an audience, where I'm sure you have a hold on them like gorilla glue bonds with wood craft. (How do you like that architect's analogy)?

Thanks for your closing line ... however, I don't want to embrace a habit, I want to embrace you! And I'm smiling.

Good night, Dear One

• • •

From: Steve
Sent: Friday, March 15, 2019 at 9:13 AM
To: Ralph
Subject: Good Morning

Hey Ralph,
Wanted to send you an e-mail thanking you for the kind letter & card! I must tell you that my Mom & also my closest friend & confidante (after many years of rebellion ...) cannot say enough of how much she is enjoying your presence in her life. I can literally hear her joy & excitement through the phone lines & this makes me incredibly happy!

I'm sure we will get to know each other more in the future but thank you again!!!

Steve

From: RALPH
Sent: Saturday, March 16, 2019 at 2:28 PM
To: Steve
Subject: Re: Good Morning

Hello Steve,
This is to acknowledge your email of yesterday. Finding it when I came home last night (rather late for me) was such a pleasant moment. It was kind of you to express your feelings regarding the friendship that has developed between Roz and me.

Upon first meeting her we shared the typical pleasantries, but the more we talked it was apparent that we both had some significant common interests. From that a deeper friendship has developed, initiating a wonderful email and telephone correspondence. And I'm very pleased about the spiritual lift it has given each of us.

Thank you for writing. I hope you and I do meet one of these days, enabling us to get acquainted.

Sincerely,
Ralph

. . .

From: RALPH
Sent: Saturday, March 16, 2019 at 4:31 PM
To: Roz
Subject: Just want to be in touch

Hi Presch,
Back online, after an active day for my granddaughter ... with love and squalor! That last part is something I plagiarized from "Nine Stories" by J.D. Salinger. You're well read and probably recognize it. If not, ask your grandkids about it. They may be old enough to be one of the generations that thrived on Salinger's literature. The striking story among the nine stories is "A Perfect Day for Bananafish".

Last evening, I had dinner with Mori's family, which caused me to get home later than usual. When I got to my emails, I was delighted to find a message from Steve. With gratitude he kindly acknowledged the letter and card I sent him, but he was kinder in telling me of his chats with you and recognizing in your voice and spirit an exhilaration coming from your comments regarding our relationship. That exchange, making him very happy, makes me very happy too. I do hope to meet him and get acquainted one of these days.

I am confident that you know the pleasure of our relationship is not one-sided. I'm really happy about the warmth shared between us. My days are peppered with thoughts of you, how you are feeling and what you're doing. (That's hot pepper, by the way)! I keep wondering when and how I can set up another visit with you, preferably where you are. It will happen, but meanwhile I am loving the connections we have via phone and email. The former is the best means because I get to hear your voice, and the excitement in it.

Mori took a couple pix of me because Calvin wanted one to use in the church newsletter. It's related to my new status as a deacon in the congregation. Anyway, despite the fact you already have enough images of me, I've decided to send these … you can choose if either is worthy of being in your collection.

I wrote back to Steve, and now have written you, and I'm suffering keyboard overkill. So, I know you'll understand as I go off-line. Gone but not forgetting you!

Ral…………………………………………

From: Roz
Sent: Saturday, March 16, 2019 at 5:26 PM
To: RALPH
Subject: Your communication is the perfect medicine for me!

Dear Dear You,
The best laid plans … I am a bit under the weather with a mean respiratory bug that captured me Thursday evening and has not given me a fever break for 3 days. I spoke to the doctor this morning, and she prescribed a Zpak to help me fight this condition. A friend picked up the script and chicken soup so I will recover in time. I am drinking so much water that floating has replaced perambulation!

Karen has been in touch (had to talk her out of getting on a plane earlier today … bless her heart) as has Steve with sympathy … a tincture of time aka days to feel the cure looks like the plan for me. I am rarely sick, so this happening brings me up short.

I am so delighted that Steve and you have emailed ... know he was impressed with your "thank you" to him. Assuming the chocolate bundt was a yummy success last night. I think the top picture Mori snapped of you is very You! It is great!!! Very HAPPY to add these to my Collection ... thank you for sharing!

I am thinking about you and sending warmest hugs (not contagious ones!!!)!

Presch

PS ... sadly I am missing the Ballet Performance tonight.

Sent from my iPhone

From: RALPH
Sent: Saturday, March 16, 2019 at 11:33 PM
To: Roz
Subject: Re: Your communication is the perfect medicine for me!

Hi Roz,
Hey, I'm so sorry to find out you're "under the weather" lately. And that it's taken control of you for a few days now. Wish I could give you some of my chicken soup ... the ideal cure! Perhaps your greatest loss from all this is missing the Ballet performance.

I know they say that drinking lots of fluid is important but be cautious with drinking all that water or you will be floating!

In an effort to get you over this "downer" I've been looking for something to send you that will make you feel better. Now I think I've found the perfect item which I'll acquire and send. I'll attach a picture to see if it will suit you. Let me know if I should send it Priority!

Now it's gotten late, I'm tired, so I'm going to do what's good for me. I'm letting you know you'll find me "under the blankets".
If you feel badly, I feel badly. I probably shouldn't make light of the situation, but my thought is that maybe laughter is the best medicine.

Praying you'll be better very soon.
Ralph

From: Roz
Sent: Sunday, March 17, 2019 at 4:58 PM
To: RALPH
Subject: Beauteous Nature!

Thank you bringing so much beauty into my life in so many meaningful ways!

Yours and only Yours,
Flaminga

From: RALPH
Sent: Sunday, March 17, 2019 at 6:10 PM
To: Roz
Subject: Re: Beauteous Nature!

Flaminga, dear,
Like any self-respecting flamingo, I expect you will resume being "in the pink" soon! The flora in your entry area are lovely, but not near so lovely as you!

You were correct, Muriel was married to Seymour ... at least there was one reference to "Mrs. Glass". However, it could be they registered as a married couple, respecting social mores of that era.

With love,
The Answer Man

From: RALPH
Sent: Sunday, March 17, 2019 at 9:31 PM
To: Roz
Subject: Re: My studio

Hi again,
When sending my last email, I failed to include a couple of pictures of my work area. Thought you might be interested in seeing where I design and draw. These are hot out of the camera ... taken this afternoon.

I continue to pray for your return to good health and high spirits.

Deacon-in-Charge

From: Roz
Sent: Sunday, March 17, 2019 at 9:56 PM
To: RALPH
Subject: Re: My studio

I am so DELIGHTED to see the sunny, airy space that nurtures your creativity! Am guessing that because I have a fever tonight (dog gone it/ damn it!!) I may be seeing your surroundings a bit blurry ... No worries because the fact that you are sharing your space with me (reflecting productivity with neat stacks and surfaces covered with potential new design expressions yet to be birthed) is worth so very much!

Thank YOU!
Beyond beyond ...

PS ... my doctor called to check on me an hour or so ago and wants to see me in the morning. Am thinking this virus is Happy in my body. It just doesn't want to leave! Bummer ...

From: RALPH
Sent: Sunday, March 17, 2019 at 10:33 PM
To: Roz
Subject: Re: My studio

That last line of your message is so perceptive. Happy in your body ... yes, lucky virus!

· · ·

From: Roz
Sent: Monday, March 18, 2019 at 10:39 AM
To: RALPH
Subject: Hooray! On the mend!

Dearest Deacon,
I knew your prayers and "etc" would work their magic! The doctor hears no congestion in my lungs and with no fever this morning (I did jump for joy) pronounced me on the mend. Cautioned me to rest for the

next two days since constant fever for 5 days is very debilitating, cough drops, and fluids will help me through the next stage of this mean virus ... drum roll please: I will be good as new!

Thank you for "being so you"!

Happy Hugs to You ... with much more to discuss!
Can almost see you smiling!

Sent from my iPhone

From: RALPH
Sent: Monday, March 18, 2019 at 4:06 PM
To: Roz
Subject: Re: Hooray! On the mend!

Dear Object of my Affection,
Your message was music to my ears. I'm so pleased that you've overcome the virus and resting now will bring you back to normal. Recovery from illness is a gift beyond treasure. Welcome back!

For all you mean to me, one would presume I would respond instantly with joy about your message. However, I was out for lunch with Mori today, to talk at some length. Yesterday marked the 2nd year since his mother's death, but because he and I were both committed to other functions, we couldn't honor the day, and met today instead. I know you understand the circumstances.

On now to another serious topic. Roz, you are now a special part of my life and as such we have talked quite candidly about a lot of personal things. I like that forthrightness, though I have to admit I sometimes let it get out of hand. Last night as I slipped into bed, I was happy you had called, and I'm grateful for your clear-headed attitude about my responsibilities. Thank you for holding the line regarding my liberal disclosures about intimate behavior. That may be a strong component of my being, but it's not something I should be revealing to you. My willingness to express my intimate nature comes from self-confidence, and the self-confidence comes from physical pride. But that doesn't excuse it! By our talking as we did last night, you made me realize I have a haughty attitude in me, and I'm informed enough to accept the fact it's indefensible when conversing with someone with your high standards, sensitivity in all levels of discourse, blessed with a depth of serious propriety, and still holding on to your love for the soulmate with whom you shared your life. Furthermore, you reminded me that my status now as a Deacon in my church demands a higher level of discretion and respectability, personal characteristics I invalidated by my loose talk.

It's with personal shame that I'm moved to apologize to you. From now on I will do my best to keep such thoughts to myself, determined to avoid embarrassing you as I must have.

I'm feeling badly about all this, but hopeful that I can salvage some admiration from you regarding many other things we can continue to enjoy … but assuredly on a higher intellectual plateau. There's not much more for me to say right now. Just give it a little time.

Loving having you in my corner,
Ralph

From: Roz
Sent: Tuesday, March 19, 2019 at 5:16 AM
To: RALPH
Subject: My Heart is Hurting for You

Yes, I am writing to you at 4:44 am this Tuesday morning … I am awakened thinking of you with a pain in my heart. You are being very harsh on yourself, and I feel for you as you self-reflect on this sense of yourself. I respect you for wanting to grapple with your sense of "imperfection" which I do not agree is an imperfection. The whole of you that you have shared with me indicates your physicality being an essential part of the being that has come to mean so very much to me. Confidence and self-assurance emanate from you as strengths to admire and inspire … the libidinous drive that contributes to your professional and creative gifts … the successes you achieve in your art and architecture and in your joy of music and nature and your joie de vivre are reflections of the all of you and of course, your love of family and your church.

I implore you in your reflection to dismiss any sense of shame … so not the case! You already embody the essence of devotion and dedication with your humanness that are gifts to me and all the lives you touch. YOU have not burdened me or embarrassed me … you have given me joy and laughter and a confidante beyond beyond!! You have not damaged a millisecond of our relationship so there is no need to salvage anything. A blemish on the skin of the peach only enhances the sweetness of the taste.

To me, You are the You I have deep feelings for and will continue to learn from and enjoy for as long as you are willing and desirous of our special connection.

Yours,
Roz

Sent from my iPad

From: RALPH
Sent: Tuesday, March 19, 2019 at 1:46 PM
To: Roz
Subject: Re: My Heart is Hurting for You

Dear, dear, Roz,
Your words are so restorative for me ... you brought me fresh tranquility with every line. Your message uplifts me so much ... yet it pains me that you were awakened by the heartache you felt, and then devoted the time to writing me.

It seems you've uncovered a characteristic of mine that I nurtured in my late high school years and carried along to the university. That is, my reflecting on the sense of myself, then working on myself to "straighten the kinks!" Or as you stated, "grappling with my imperfection". Bless you for your insight, because while I examine myself detail by detail, you judge me as a whole being of which the good features and the bad features churn, and a balanced, respectable person emerges. So, your words have transported me to a healthier state of mind.
I love your maxim about the peach but have to own up to the truth that you are the peach in our relationship ... I'm more an avocado (if you get the connection)!

I do intend to maintain our connection and strengthen it. To inform you in that regard, I had a follow-up exam with my cardiologist this morning, and the new tablet prescribed seems to have my blood pressure under control. That's normal now, and the heart rate is normal. Seems like I'm good to go.

The sun is beautiful here today and I'm soaking it up. Perhaps better to have some gloomy, cool days which will nudge me to the sunny south. Meanwhile take care of yourself ... stay as sweet as you are.

Taster

• • •

From: RALPH
Sent: Tuesday, March 19, 2019 at 4:46 PM
To: Roz
Subject: 2nd med report

Hi again,
Another bit of good news from my dermatologist this afternoon. The biopsy report came back and the spot on my scalp was benign. No worry ... no concern. I am trouble free.

My hope is that this day has turned out to be superb for you.

Your guy

From: Roz
Sent: Tuesday, March 19, 2019 at 8:18 PM
To: RALPH
Subject: Good News Day!

Dear You,
Where to begin my feeling of thankfulness? Thank you for sharing your good health news! Thank you for feeling and hearing all the messages I sent to you this early morning and thank you for being the honest man you are, recognizing your value to yourself and to me.

I began to know your introspective self during your challenging moments in the fall with your Church Project and the disappointments you shared. I listened to your humility as praise was focused on you and your accomplishments. I sensed your caring for friends in need, near and far whom you offered to help and support. I felt your love and devotion to your family adoring your many responsibilities that give you keen insight and appreciation of your granddaughters and Mori's family unit. I heard your struggle to accept decisions that were made differently from the decisions you would have made and yet you "were accepting". I felt and feel your depth of personal loss. I recognized your response to the joy of musical heights and the beauty of nature. I am in awe of your spiritual commitment to your faith and your Church that guide you and give you strength and direction ... all of these complement the multiple facets of You. So many times ... when we are alone, we lose perspective of the whole of ourselves and focus inappropriately on one facet, losing the clarity of our wholeness. I think the worry of a loss of perspective was my pain for you and hence my early morning missive.

Gee ... how did this dissertation happen ? Apologies if you zzzed a bit ...

I am very happy that we can be of lighter hearts and share our humorous and witty selves ... and feel our bond!!

Yours,
Flaminga

PS ... I directed a successful videotaping today at Palm Beach State College and was home in bed napping (doctor's orders yesterday) at 3:30. Feeling better since weakness prevails as aftermath of fever days. Should be myself in a day or two but without fever is my happy place for now.

Sent from my iPad

From: RALPH
Sent: Wednesday, March 20, 2019 at 12:28 AM
To: Roz
Subject: Re: Good News Day!

Hi Presch,
Returned home shortly ago from a church meeting tonight. The elders and deacons met collectively to review the goals set for the coming year. The goals were voted on at the annual meeting last month and approved. Now as we are at the threshold of spring, we have to prioritize the projects at the top of the list and begin to perform. Several on the list are classified as building improvements, so I know I'll have my share of scheduling and monitoring what gets done.

You are extremely gracious and positive in recounting some of my church construction activities of a year ago. A hearty thank you for the solid support you noted in recognition of my contributions. Your loving thoughts are distributed throughout this latest email, the proof of your heart of gold. I've observed it in your comments about others too (family, friends, and associates) with whom you are providing insight, or sharing expertise, or encouraging them with organized events. You really are a leader in guiding others on a creative path. I know it of course because you're my muse!

Right now, I'm losing it ... drowsy and not doing well on this keyboard. Crazy of me to claim distress when you are the one who had your rest stolen from you as you were aroused very early in the a.m. by my rattled state of mind.

Nevertheless, I have to shut down now. Will be back again tomorrow with hope of being a more refreshed correspondent.

Goodnight and good rest to you during the hours left. Don't go photographing any moon shots tonight.

Sleepy (not the dwarf)

From: Roz
Sent: Wednesday, March 20, 2019 at 11:03 AM
To: RALPH
Subject: Snow White and Her Buds!

Ohhh, the mere suggestion of the Seven Dwarfs made me smile! The very first movie I was taken to see at age 4 was "Snow White" at a very big theatre on Grand Avenue? Consequently, this experience was my introduction to imagination brought to life on a huge screen that left its indelible mark on me for only forever!

I did rest well last night and missed the beautiful full moon this cycle ... am feeling like I am in the final phase of this illness and will welcome wellness enthusiastically, very soon! Took last of the Zpak 6 pills this morning.

Forgive me, but reading about the first of your leadership meetings last night made me giggle (not regarding the seriousness of the prioritizing among the carefully selected, chosen few) but my seeing the two letters (impact of my very special close connection to you over these last 7 months) Elders and Deacons- E D... I mean no disrespect, but I had a "former Ralph Moment"!

Deep breath ... by the by, are there any female E's and D's?

I am so delighted that Karen decided to fly down to share a few days with me to celebrate our birthdays together on March 31st! After mine and before hers. If you recall, she departed quickly in January to avoid weather issues on her drive north ... so we missed girl time aka mother/daughter shopping and added togetherness. Happy we can have this time given her very busy schedule/life! It took all of my strength to convince her not to come during my illness but now it will be good!

Given all your new responsibilities, am guessing your life will quickly become quite busy, and I know you will enjoy new challenges and will jump into projects with both feet!

I am smiling for you!
Wishing you a Happy Wednesday!

Warmest hugs,
Bashful

Sent from my iPhone

From: RALPH
Sent: Wednesday, March 20, 2019 at 5:26 PM
To: Roz
Subject: Re: Snow White and Her Buds!

Good afternoon, Presch,
Hey, really good to hear from you. The best news was your improvement ... you rested well, you seem to be at the end of the illness, and you're feeling back in action. Now it's wellness, not hell-ness!

I remember that big theater on Grand Avenue. Wasn't it The St. Louis Theater, and ultimately got converted into St. Louis Symphony Hall? As a kid my oldest sister took me there from time to time. Believe it or not, I can remember once when we were passing one of those grandiose downtown theaters, and the movie poster behind the glass by the ticket booth was billing "Frenchman's Creek", with Ronald Coleman (I think). Memory's good from way back, but I can't remember what I ate for lunch!

Your mention of loving life portrayed on the big screen made me wonder what shows you've seen lately at AMC? Any new films out that got your attention and your applause?

You're forgiven! I understand your motivation to giggle when you "connected" Elders and Deacons with ED. Of course, it could also have triggered a memory of the TV show "MR. ED". As you may remember that was a horse, and you know horses don't have E-D problems. I did think you were quite perceptive to link it with Elders and Deacons. BTW, in a recent email when I stated that, in your maxim, you would be the peach ... I would more likely be an avocado. Did you interpret that, and how?

Answering your gender inquiry ... yes there are two Deaconesses.

Well, no wonder you came back to life, having Karen arrive with hugs. How lucky you are! I know you'll have some wonderful days together ... ! envy either one of you, being in the other's company. Of course, you'll greet her for me.

I had brunch with Calvin this morning, and we did cover some ground about the next opportunities for me to manage a few things. Some of it will be small potatoes, until we notice contributions are up and we can budget for a few bigger ventures.

Wednesday was "Happy" as you wished for me. It was affected somewhat because today Spring began! More-so because you delivered some charm and humor. Back atcha, dear.

Let me sign off like this:
Get real ... you're anything but Bashful hah hah hah!

. . .

From: RALPH
Sent: Friday, March 22, 2019 at 8:54 AM
To: Roz
Subject: Friday ritual

Hi Presch,
Nothing new to report. Just getting prepared to head out to Brookline.
Wanting you to know … today I'm committed to my granddaughter, but
my thoughts will be all for you.

Wide awake but dreaming …

From: Roz
Sent: Friday, March 22, 2019 at 8:54 AM
To: RALPH
Subject: Re: Friday ritual

I have had you in the front of my morning thoughts, too! The kitchen
window is open, and the sun is shining brightly in a blue cloudless sky …
the feeling of a "cold front" dipping into temps in the 60's this morning!
Am sending you a picture that expresses my missing you!

Happy times with your granddaughter making memory keepers!

My hugs to you!
Flaminga

From: Roz
Sent: Friday, March 22, 2019 at 12:46 PM
To: RALPH
Subject: For You!
Attachments: IMG_2267.jpg

Sending YOU sunshiny wishes for a day filled with loving thoughts and
laughing moments!

Sent from my iPhone

From: RALPH
Sent: Friday, March 22, 2019 at 3:53 PM
To: Roz
Subject: Re: For You!

Hey, so nice to hear from you! It's gloomy here and rainy, plus my granddaughter has a cold and is a bit out of sorts. She's napping now. Love the pic you sent ... wish I was there with you!

Displaced person.

From: Roz
Sent: Saturday, March 23, 2019 at 3:12 PM
To: RALPH
Subject: Printing Itinerary!!!

FYI ... may have to call for plastic surgery intervention to adjust facial muscles that have been frozen in a beaming smile for the last several hours ... may ask for lift and line removal while under anesthesia!

"Decided "is such a good state of being!
Presch

Sent from my iPhone

From: RALPH
Sent: Saturday, March 23, 2019 at 4:14 PM
To: Roz
Subject: Re: Reprinting Itinerary!!!

Dear to my Heart,
I thought that would be a good way to pump you up today. But don't you do anything to let them change that radiant smile you manage so easily. I'm the one who needs a transformation! (I'm working on it). It feels good to realize the plans for travel are underway. I suppose you noticed I added a couple days to this trip. I'm looking forward to that extra time together.

You noted "Decided" so well and so succinctly. Forget MA and FL. Decided is the state I wanna be in.

Gadfly

From: RALPH
Sent: Sunday, March 24, 2019 at 12:23 AM
To: Roz
Subject: Attached is the music program of this evening

Hi Roz,

I'm certain you are sleeping now. Sorry I didn't get this to you earlier, but I've been busy in the kitchen preparing food for tomorrow's noon dinner. I'm hosting Mori's family for the afternoon. It will be good for all of them to get away for a change and have some fun together without using their own time to arrange and manage everything. It will be my home cooking (roast pork tenderloin, au gratin potatoes, 3 or 4 veggies, and I will finish with my oversized apple tart which the girls love) instead of the sushi platter which they usually bring when they furnish the food.

The hosts for the gathering this evening did a superb presentation. There were about 75 people in attendance, a fine food buffet, and an open bar with a collection of wines. Everyone seemed to be having a good time socializing.

The soloist, a soprano, is a regular member of the Camerata performers, and she was excellent. I would judge her to be about 35 years old. She's an immigrant from Colombia, S.A. and has an amazing voice. It's clear as a bell, with a remarkable range, and she has perfect control.

She was dressed so appropriately for this event, wearing a one-piece blouse/pants combination (the pant legs were cut full, so when they hung side by side, they gave an appearance of a gown).

A kind of pleated waistband joined the blouse and pants together. I suppose there was a zipper up the back to allow her to slip into it. She really looked great, sort of dressy/casual for that type of party performance.

Well, it's gotten late, and I'm going to have a busy day tomorrow with church and family dinner, so I'm going to close. I will probably be getting in touch with you tomorrow evening when "the dust has settled". Have a good Sunday. Hugs!

High Society Reporter

From: Roz
Sent: Tuesday, March 26, 2019 at 6:59 PM
To: RALPH
Subject: Ahhh ...

Houston, we may have a problem ... need your voice of reason.

Dilemmenus

Sent from my iPhone

From: RALPH
Sent: Tuesday, March 26, 2019 at 10:35 PM
To: Roz
Subject: Re: Ahhh ...

Just found your message. Are you still up and around?

Solveallus

• • •

From: Roz
Sent: Wednesday, March 27, 2019 at 11:24 AM
To: RALPH
Subject: Happy to be "on the same page with you"!

Just finished a long, fun conversation with a very special friend of long
history, and I want to share with you when next we chat. I realized a
chapter I haven't talked to you about (amazing since we have talked
about soooo much and soooo many topics) ... am jotting this to you so
you can remind me about this New Orleans moment.

Happy Wednesday ... hope you are feeling Spring in the air in
sunny temps.

Decided and Embracing the Now

Sent from my iPad

From: RALPH
Sent: Wednesday, March 27, 2019 at 12:54 PM
To: Roz
Subject: Re: Happy to be "on the same page with you"!

I do not understand these damn iPhones. I had a fairly long reply to your email on screen and then must have touched a wrong key. It all disappeared, and I tried to retrieve it, but nothing worked. So, I'm getting off this thing. I don't have time for this! Sorry, will talk later.

• • •

From: Roz
Sent: Thursday, March 28, 2019 at 8:34 AM
To: RALPH
Subject: In Technicolor!

Dear Flamingo,
Thank you for mailing your "real" Jet Blue Confirmation to me! Your visit is a gift to US! I am so happy to anticipate shared time and new "memory keepers" we will make together! Sweet anticipation is the modus operandi for now and for the next weeks!

Smiling...
Flaminga

Sent from my iPhone

From: RALPH
Sent: Thursday, March 28, 2019 at 11:15 PM
To: Roz
Subject: Re: In Technicolor!

Dear Flaminga,
Good grief, I can't believe I've used up all the day and not gotten back to you! I found your email after finishing my morning ritual and came into the room to get some tidy whiteys on my body, then the phone rang ... it was the electrician who is scheduled to do a bit more work at the church. I decided I better eat and get moving, but when I checked the fridge, it was near empty, so I put more clothes on and headed for the market and things just got worse after that. Back home after five, I began to prepare a

new dinner menu for me. It was fresh squid which looked so good, and a small-enough pack that I could eat all of it for dinner. It took me a while to prepare, and by the time I finished and cleaned up the kitchen, it was 10 p.m. After going through the mail and closing down the living quarters, I'm back upstairs and in my tidy whiteys again. Shall I send a picture?

I'm glad you reported about the Jet Blue confirmation. I forgot about mailing that to you. Yes, it will be "sweet anticipation" on both ends of the flight route. I think I'm going to be restless during those three hours of flight time! Waiting to hear how West Side Story delivered. If they had a good cast, it's near impossible to ruin the music and dance presentation. I hope you're still humming those lyrics.

Now on to bed. Got to be prepared for Brookline tomorrow.

Flamingo

• • •

From: Roz
Sent: Saturday, March 30, 2019 at 8:48 AM
To: RALPH
Subject: Good Morning!

Having coffee with you this morning ... please, tell me the story (you always have a story, happily) about the stamps on the precious 5x7 manila envelope. The antique piano surrounded by "Peace unites a nation like harmony in music" ... true message of the universal connection music can achieve!!! And your display in horizontal positioning, of the five Bicentennial stamps quoting the Preamble to the Constitution ... so much to take in after the first blush of happiness I feel recognizing your perfect penmanship and return address sticker!!!

Earth to Roz ...

Sent from my iPhone

From: RALPH
Sent: Saturday, March 30, 2019 at 1:46 PM
To: Roz
Subject: Re: Good Morning!

Dear ... you know,
You are precious and so are your morning moments with me. I hope coffee with me made it sweeter! And your sign-off was a gem.

The story of the stamps is both amusing and sad. It relates to my sister again ... the middle sister who wanted greatly to amass a fortune. (I can't fault her, she did pretty well). As a young woman she got hooked on the U.S. Postal Service promoting "buy stamps" and reap the fortune later. Diligently she went and got first-day issues and a full sheet of each of those stamps. Fast-forward now to old age (let's say 85 years, she lived to be 93) and she's reviewing her assets. She decided stamp-collecting was too much of a nuisance. She decided to share some of what she had with her closest relatives, so she sent me several sheets of different designs, of which you just received some. When she died, her attorney and I were named co-administrators of her Trust. We reviewed her assets and found the box of stamp sheets.

We had a philatelist count and evaluate the collection and it came to a little over $12,000. The attorney knew about the spring stamp market, so we put the collection there for sale. It was looked over by many but the highest bid we got for all of it was $600. We liquidated it just so we didn't have to devote anymore time and cost to it. Referring to the antique piano stamp on the envelope ... did you see the denomination? ... 8-3/4 cents.

Thinking back on your email of yesterday and your comments when we talked on the phone, I appreciate all the favor you've shown me. I'm so happy if I can please you.

We're enjoying temps in the 60's today, and I saw daffodils nosing up through the leaves on the ground. Shall I start planting the petunias?

Got to go to the laundry, almost out of shirts. Will talk again soon.

Over'n Out

• • •

From: Roz
Sent: Sunday, March 31, 2019 at 3:33 PM
To: RALPH
Subject: Thinking of You!

Just want you to know you are very present wherever I am!

Happy Sunday!!

Sent from my iPhone

From: RALPH
Sent: Sunday, March 31, 2019 at 5:02 PM
To: Roz
Subject: Re: Thinking of You!

Spectacular! Oh, what a choice pair you are! It could only be better if I were there between you.

It's obvious how happy both you and your daughter are being together. A pity that you only have a few days to cover all the stuff there is to chat about. Make the most of it.

My Sunday was wonderful. Up early and a great breakfast, uplifting church service, then an afternoon hospital visit with a church friend. He's an older gent and doesn't get many visitors. So my coming cheered him.

I picked up a few things at the store and just arrived home. Now it's time for a bite to eat, but when finding your picture I had to write first. Roz you look fabulous ... really breathtaking. Thanks for capturing that moment or as you would say, "it's beyond beyond!"

A big hug from me for Karen. Love to you. Will talk to you again soon.

Ralph

From: Roz
Sent: Sunday, March 31, 2019 at 9:31 PM
To: RALPH
Subject: Spreading your Special Cheer!

So nice to read of your hospital visit. It is always so gratifying when we extend ourselves knowing we have brought comfort to someone in need ... I know your warmth and caring conversation made your friend feel so much better.

Karen and I have had a fun day with non-stop talking and catching up ... because her flight was early this morning, she is tired and needs to get to bed for much needed zzzzs ...

With a moment to reflect, I want you to know I spoke at length about my growing feelings for you and she was so thrilled ... looking into her eyes made me know All is right with the world ...

Smiling ... am guessing you are too!

Sent from my iPhone

From: RALPH
Sent: Sunday, March 31, 2019 at 10:45 PM
To: Roz
Subject: Re: Spreading your Special Cheer!

It's pitch dark outside, but there's "sunshine" in my office now. Such a treat to find your message.

For the past hour or more, I was writing a letter of response to a 2nd or 3rd cousin in Germany who wrote to me (probably a month ago) but to whom I've failed to reply. I decided tonight I HAD to get with it! So moving right along, or at least I thought so, this computer of mine started hanging-up, doing nothing for about 10 seconds, then continued with my message. After about 15 minutes of that, I went to "Restart", got up and went to get a drink. When I got back, the machine was up and running again, and most importantly you were in my inbox. Could I have had a wider smile???

Regarding my hospitalized friend, you had it right ... he was so happy when I walked into the lounge where he was alone, perusing a book,

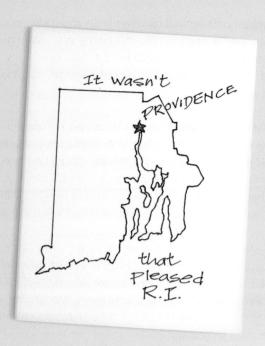

It wasn't PROVIDENCE

that
Pleased
R.I.

It was a special
person that
caught my eye!

Day by day I'm
having more
fun getting
to know you Roz!

Ralph

looking dreary. He lighted up with a smile and gave me a warm embrace. I was with him for nearly two hours of enjoyable chatting, then I begged off because I had to get a few items from the store for my dinner. He thanked me, told me he expects to get released this coming Tuesday, and he can't wait!

I envy the hours you and Karen had together. I could see from that picture you were having a splendid time. Both of you looked radiant, a sight to behold! I'm so glad you spoke with Karen about how we feel, and she apparently showed her pleasure about the enthusiasm you and I have for each other. It's relieving that she responded positively. Yes, I am smiling due to that news.

Well, I better get back to my German cousin, so that letter goes out tomorrow. More than likely, tomorrow looms large for you, with many things the two of you will be doing. Make the most of it. I on the other hand will probably be staying here at home, lots of piddly things to get out of my way. Loved hearing from you. Now, you've earned some zzzzzzzzzzz's for yourself.

Good night.
Ralph

PS - Your Times clipping came today too. Expressive piece. I think I know whom you had in mind.

• • •

From: RALPH
Sent: Monday, April 1, 2019 at 4:44 PM
To: Roz
Subject: USPS Priority Delivery

Boola Boola, Boola Boola ... Presch sent me a new spatula!

I shall wield it with aplomb,
Skilled by what I learned from Mom.

Cookies ... sure, I'll make a batch.
You can help or sit and watch.

Take a moment, note my name,
I'm headed for the Hall of Fame!

Chef Raoul

There you did it again, flamingoing me into oblivion! I'm crying "fowl"!

I went to the front door to check the temperature outdoors, and there was your box at my feet.

I love such surprises, wondered what it could be, and opened it immediately. It's a perfect utensil for all the mixing, folding, and churning I do in the batter bowl, plus it's equipped with a stiff wood handle instead of the typical flimsy plastic version. We don't like plastic ... flowers or otherwise!

Thanks. You made my day.

• • •

From: RALPH
Sent: Monday, April 1, 2019 at 5:34 PM
To: Roz
Subject: West Side Story

Back again,
You were again so thoughtful, sending the copy of the "West Side Story" program to me. I hadn't given it much attention when I opened the box, but just now I took time to read about the production.

The director, Marcos Santana, was quite imaginative and innovative with his opening and closing sequences of the performance. In his discussion with the reporter who interviewed him, he explained his concept for focusing on an old Maria at the opening of the show, reflecting in retrospect on the events that stole the love between her and Tony. Then after the main plot of the story is over, as an ending Santana concentrates on old Maria again (never having married after her loss of Tony) with her being back in Puerto Rico, surviving the terrible hurricane that inundated the island. That fresh approach conceptually gives a new perception of the story, so I'm wondering is that how Santana actually staged it? And if so, do you feel it was successful in this production?

This is your High Society Reporter writing now.

From: Roz
Sent: Monday, April 1, 2019 at 10:37 PM
To: RALPH
Subject: Reluctant to Call ... too late an hour?

Dear Dear,
Since you mentioned awakening early this morning and being tired earlier, I think I better not call tonight.

The Symphony was beautiful, and Karen was mesmerized as was I listening to a remarkable pianist play Brahms 2nd piano Concerto in B flat Major!!!!

More details when next we speak? Wishing you the best of dreams!

Flaminga

Sent from my iPhone

From: RALPH
Sent: Tuesday, April 2, 2019 at 11:56 AM
To: Roz
Subject: Re: Reluctant to Call ... too late an hour?

Hi Presch,
Thank you for your sense of reasoning and for not calling last night. I was tired and slipped into bed at 9:45 p.m. That's the last thing I remember until I awoke for a bathroom call around 4:00 a.m.

Now I have to run over to the church, to lock up after a plumber's visit this morning. I'll get back to you later. Thanks for your understanding.

Deac-on duty

• • •

From: Roz
Sent: Tuesday, April 2, 2019 at 11:40 PM
To: RALPH
Subject: Success!

I am guessing you are asleep so I will just think/speak quietly in whispers to you since I am missing our conversations. I respect your decision not to call while Karen is here, but I do miss our happy ramblings...yes, Karen Jet Blues back to Logan tomorrow night. We plan to do a bit more shopping tomorrow, and I want to take her to lunch at a unique spot she has not yet experienced.

We have had long talks, in between her client calls and work time, and I think she has welcomed the change of scene and pace for this short respite. Being here for her is a relaxing time sans long commutes and the bumper to bumper traffic of a metropolis. She is always so amused listening to my daily dynamics. The scenic cast of characters are a constant source of interest to her as she marvels at my busyness. She has been so helpful with computer/techie issues and we have chatted about summer plans ... too many unanswerable questions that leave me in bit of a quandary ... both Karen and I are happiest when our organizational needs are fulfilled, but life doesn't always cooperate so frustrating moments are inevitable. I keep reminding myself to focus on the "now". We have talked at length about the future and the possibilities of being closer to each other in two demographics based on seasons ... we will see. I so enjoy our shared time and recognize (with giggles) how frequently roles reverse ... having mutual respect and admiration for one another is very special and we know how lucky we are despite rare mother/daughter moments when we disagree. Fortunately laughter and humor are constants and being together is important for us. Fun times are not to be taken for granted ...

Thanks for letting me bend your ear, hypothetically speaking ... happy dreams.

Sent from my iPad

From: RALPH
Sent: Wednesday, April 3, 2019 at 1:09 PM
To: Roz
Subject: Re: Success!

Dear Presch,
Not only are you precious, you're also special! The evidence of that keeps popping up, and I am so blessed to be exposed to it.
I believe I must have heard your "[quiet] whispers", for I slept well and arose comfortable and rested. It was still only 3 a.m. so after my brief "relief", I returned to bed and sank back into sleep. The morning sunshine was bright and awakened me again. At that moment I was feeling on top of the world. After my shower and devotions, I clicked into the secular world of the internet. There I found treasure!

Your message revealed how intermingled you and Karen are, comfortably buoyant about the moments you savor, and sadly resolute in acceptance of the inescapable times when you must be apart. You made it clear how deprived you feel by those occasions of separation. I'm grateful for your willingness to include me in disclosing such emotional "downers" because it strengthens my own resolve to calmly accept similar circumstances in my own life.

You wrote so beautifully about your relationship, and the love you share. Though you sometimes disagree, it's never contentious and never diminishes the love and respect you have in your heart. I'm simply envious of your well grounded state of mind…a characteristic of yours that has become rooted in my mind and has guaranteed my trust in you.

Everything you wrote was serious, but light enough to be relaxed and conversational, and wonderfully literate. Truly you are a fine writer. I'm still learning from you!

You may bend my ear anytime, for you never shout into it. You only lavish me with quiet whispers!

You Make Me Feel So Young (Sung to the tune of "You Make Me Feel So Young")

• • •

From: Roz
Sent: Wednesday, April 3, 2019 at 11:06 PM
To: RALPH
Subject: Pasta dinner

Delish ... the aroma is scrumptious! Like the pasta shape (name?) ... Are there black mussels ? mushrooms? Can't tell. Definitely deserves coverage by gourmet critic ... inspired Italian moment! Yum ...

Leftovers tomorrow?

Sent from my iPhone

From: RALPH
Sent: Wednesday, April 3, 2019 at 11:24 PM
To: Roz
Subject: re: Pasta dinner

Would you believe ... I've been trying since I got off the phone with you to send this photo? Incredulous!

Well there it is. Barilla's "campanelle" pasta, which is my choice (the recipe I have calls for spaghetti or linguine). In a skillet I sauté chopped green pepper, 1 large garlic clove minced, 5 white button mushrooms sliced, and 9 shrimp together in butter and olive oil. Then after 11 minutes in boiling water, drain the pasta, put back in the pot, combine the sauté contents into the pasta, and mix all the contents. Put in bowl, sprinkle with grated romano/parmesan cheese and fresh ground black pepper. Ummmmmmmm! No wine. I drink mineral water.

I noticed your email response to the photo, so apparently one of my attempts to get it to you worked. Tomorrow I take my iPhone out and throw it under the bus!

From: RALPH
Sent: Wednesday, April 3, 2019 at 11:28 PM
To: Roz
Subject: re: Pasta dinner

Happy to know it looked good to you. Regrettably no leftovers ... but I could do it all over again. Well worth it!

From: Roz
Sent: Thursday, April 4, 2019 at 8:34 AM
To: RALPH
Subject: On behalf of your iPhone ...

Oh, I certainly share your frustration when technology does not behave as we expect it to (given our limited skills as a generational old fogey) ... but, please spare the phone for the sake of our connectivity!

Your sense of humor and cleverness are two of your most endearing personality "profiles" and I would be forlorn if any part of you (via any technology) went (aka thrown) under the bus! ! !

Deep breaths and one more for good measure saves us from actions we may regret! So ... please handle your phone with TLC and keep all systems functioning at least until 4/27!

Now best to "laugh out loud"/lol!

Wishing you a happy Spring day!

PS ... love reading your step by step recipe a la Chef Raoul ... life these days is so much better sharing it with you!!

Hugs to You

From: RALPH
Sent: Thursday, April 4, 2019 at 4:56 PM
To: Roz
Subject: Re: On behalf of your iPhone ...

This morning I got out of bed, looked at my iPhone and smiled. All is forgiven! Don't have time to hold grudges. I took your advice ... took some deep breaths ... then took a shower!

Out of the shower I found a new email from an old school friend from my hometown. He married a girl in our class, one who was an adventuresome type, and they are both still living, and roaming the country. They bought one of those camper units that you hitch up behind a pick-up truck, then go investigate every back road across the U.S. Not my sort of life ... "on the road again, I just can't wait to get on the road again ... " (thank you Willie).

Now that I've got that out of the way, the meat of his message was that he's having a hip replacement next week. He doesn't seem a bit worried about the procedure despite his 52 year-old son having had a hip replaced recently, which was unsuccessful because the pelvic socket was too large for the femur. So now the son is waiting for an open date to have his "replacement" replaced. There comes Murphy's Law again.

This fellow has a cache of photos from our elementary school days too, so he attached a few to see if I could remember the occasions we were enjoying when the pics were taken. I do remember, and brace yourself, it was 72 years ago.

Look down the rows and see if you can spot me. Look for the scrawny kid with his shoulders slumped. I emailed my friend back, updating him about my life these days. After my wife died, they were very supportive, invited me to go along on one of their camper trips and continue to check in with me every so often to see how I'm doing. I've told them I'm doing rather well now, but I haven't given them any indication of what is giving me new life these days. The truism that "life is so much better now, sharing it with you" is kept close to my heart. For now I think it's prudent to be selfish and keep it off "the grapevine".

I've got to stop now. I do hope you are busy enough to take your mind off living solo. It won't be too long. I'll be back later.

Sorry, I've tried to attach a couple pics but am unsuccessful. I've been wanting to send this for an hour, so I'm going to do that, and I'll try to get the pics to you later.

● ● ●

To Rosalind from RHI

FINDING SERENITY

Deep thoughts constantly engulf my mind,
Inclined to expression of ideals I must fulfill.
Layered one on one, beyond all measure of mankind,
Your presence in my life keeps me decidedly tranquil.

March 25, 2019

From: Roz
Sent: Thursday, April 4, 2019 at 11:11 PM
To: RALPH
Subject: "Finding Serenity"

I meant to tell you earlier how often I read your poem and how meaningful it is to me to think that I can fulfill a need for you that gives you strength. The depth of your introspection that leads you positively to your truer self is admirable.

You honor me with your words that touch my heart.

Sent from my iPhone

From: RALPH
Sent: Friday, April 5, 2019 at 11:34 AM
To: Roz
Subject: Re: "Finding Serenity"

Coming from you, that warms my heart. You can't imagine how much I value your presence in my life ... how much my thoughts dwell with you. Aside from the love of my life, I have never had any evidence of those around me taking notice of my deeper emotions. I am amazed that you have come along now and recognize what I need. You are one more of God's blessings.

• • •

From: RALPH
Sent: Friday, April 5, 2019 at 9:29 PM
To: Roz
Subject: Praise youth!

Hi Roz,
With all thanks to Mori, here are the pictures I wanted to send you. These were taken when I was in the 8th grade. That was in 1948. Can you find "yours truly" in the pack?

Small town guy

From: Roz
Sent: Friday, April 5, 2019 at 9:56 PM
To: RALPH
Subject: Am Guessing ...

In the top picture, I think you may be the cute fella sitting in the grass in the 1st row 5th from the left ... but maybe you may be the last guy on the right??? No, think you are #5??? In the second picture you might be the 2nd from the right kneeling in the 1st row ... maybe ???

Sent from my iPhone

From: RALPH
Sent: Friday, April 5, 2019 at 10:15 PM
To: Roz
Subject: Re: Am Guessing ...

OK, super sleuth! You got both of them right. Now I'm going to take a look at your entries.

From: Roz
Sent: Friday, April 5, 2019 at 10:05 PM
To: RALPH
Subject: Me in 1948 at age 6

Actually 7 years old!!

From: RALPH
Sent: Friday, April 5, 2019 at 10:25 PM
To: Roz
Subject: Re: Me in 1948 at age 6

Well, you really were a little cutie weren't you, and you had already cultivated that winning smile. Your father must have loved you so much. Now I'm the one who benefits!

• • •

From: RALPH
Sent: Saturday, April 6, 2019 at 10:02 PM
To: Roz
Subject: Dinner Tonight

Hi Presch,
Had a late dinner tonight. Just finished cleaning up the kitchen, thought I better connect with you. Oh yeah, the menu, it was steak filet (provided by Mori), with Frenchy home fries, summer squash and green pepper combo, and white button mushrooms ... tasty! Dessert was my two meds seen in the lower right corner of the pic.

I'm getting off here now. Will call you in a few minutes.

Food 'n Foto Guy

• • •

From: RALPH
Sent: Sunday, April 7, 2019 at 9:18 AM
To: Roz
Subject: Getting spiritual

Hi Presch,
Now I'm fresh ... just out of my shower. Looking myself over I see a creaky declining man, but I can see minute details of the boy in the schoolyard. Despite the features of aging, I see a creation that is beautiful. You are instrumental in my shift in thinking about this. I'm happily absorbed into the world of "the creation" all around me ... here, today, it's about sun and clear blue skies and thanking God for all He has provided. In an hour

or so I'll be in a consecrated environment, immersed in thoughts of my better self due to my faith. You are a positive influence. I'll be deeply into thoughts of you too. I cherish this moment in the long course of my life. I am blessed. I pray that you feel sanctity in this day too.

Ralph

• • •

From: Roz
Sent: Tuesday, April 9, 2019 at 2:40 PM
To: RALPH
Subject: Mindscapes ...

Just home from spending 2hours (!?@&!!) waiting for regular Toyota Maintenance (friendly guys in accommodating mode but "apologetically backed up"!). Now I am ready to drive the highways and the byways in June ... seriously thinking about driving up to Boston with scenic "friend stops" along the miles ... want to be my road mate? After last summer you probably don't fancy a long driving trip. It is likely I am slightly delusional but think it may a good idea to have wheels to visit friends in New England during the summer months rather than depend on Karen's generosity of time or the train (have been a passenger to NY and CT often in past summers).

Karen will probably talk me out of this plan ... it's fun imagining plans until reality (aka Karen or Steve) jostles my ideas. Good thing I am so adaptable!

FYI ... froze remaining applesauce for you to taste (also useful for pill swallowing) ...

Sending this with a smile because the more we know about each other the more there is to smile about ... agree?

Hope the lectern is progressing ... hope the expert lectern creator is happy ...

Sent from my iPhone

Dear Cell Phone,
I pride myself on being "a problem solver" and acknowledge being a bit
shaky about "solving puzzles" with the exception of puzzles that have
pieces that fit together to make the whole! Many a New Hampshire
tabletop supported puzzles with umpteen pieces for extended periods
of time over the years ...

I am, however, joyously reassured that the "lectern creator is happy"!!!

I appreciate your feedback regarding a long distance drive through
scenic vistas and trafficked challenges ... more likely I will rent
wheels once I am in the northeast as the need arises ... I do value
independence but could be talked out of too much of such should the
right circumstance present itself ...

Oh, contraire ... please do lecture me! Your articulation is always
special and unique!

Am ambivalent about my afternoon Grievance Committee Meeting
today with two hearings to "adjudicate" ... ugh. Happy Wednesday of
creativity and project accomplishment and worthy Bible Study tonight
... both promising you beneficial outcomes!

Enjoy these positive moments.
Bye for now

• • •

From: RALPH
Sent: Saturday, April 13, 2019 at 9:35 PM
To: Roz
Subject: Results
Attatchment: lectern.jpg

Hi Roz,
Drum roll please, not because it's great, but because it's done! I'm about
to eat something. I'll call you in a bit. If you don't want to wait up, just send
me an email. I'll get to you tomorrow.
Waiting to hear what you think!

Speaker of the House

From: Roz
Sent: Saturday, April 13, 2019 at 9:40 PM
To: RALPH
Subject: Re: Results

Stunning ... and the classic clean lines inspire the observer! YES!!!
Calvin will love it!!!!

Sent from my iPhone

From: Roz
Sent: Sunday, April 14, 2019 at 2:50 PM
To: RALPH
Subject: Re: Results

Dear You,
I have been able to think of little else today other than THE LECTERN!
Perhaps for you today was/is focused on prayer and spiritual
inspiration and realistically Calvin will not see your beautifully
crafted model until the work week begins ... if that's the case ... all good
things come to those who wait ...

Really have been marveling at your days/weeks of disciplined focus
to patiently create an exact representation of your lectern research
and studied details ... and to have given the long hours to this project
refining it as only you can do ... so impresses me!! Sigh ...

lectern.jpg

When next we talk, remind me to tell you about my friend in New Orleans ...

Hope you are having a sunny Sunday.
Me

Sent from my iPhone

From: RALPH
Sent: Sunday, April 14, 2019 at 8:55 PM
To: Roz
Subject: Re: Lectern on my mind ...

Dear Me,
You're kind to write me about my lectern project ... that you've continued to concentrate on the various issues with which I was dealing. It may very well seem like overkill for me to examine and re-examine simple details, but it gives me peace of mind, that just as the whole thing becomes reality, some silly feature won't appear to haunt me every time I see it in use.

With my confidence rather high about pleasing Calvin with the results, I began a conversation with him in the fellowship hall after the service and used my iPhone to pull up the pictures I took last night. He was amazed with what he saw and asked who made the mock-up. That it was I surprised him, and he was asking how, and with whom I made it.

The upshot of it all was he really likes it. I explained it was important for him to see it and touch it, to judge it for comfort since he'll be the primary user. Reviewing the pictures of the model, I pointed out what I thought was a too large tablet on the top, and the tablet should be lowered a few inches (we can decide that when he is standing at the lectern). He will be coming to my home tomorrow to look everything over and then turn it over to the wood craftsman. I think I was buoyant last night after completing my project, plus having the added bonus of a conversation with you before I closed down for the night. I did not sleep soundly, was up for a couple bathroom visits, and finally found myself wide awake at 4:15 a.m. I'm feeling the loss of sleep now and not sure I'll be able to hang on for "Les Misérables". Well, can catch the Tuesday night replay on PBS.

Loved hearing from you. Sorry I delayed responding due to my chauffeur activity with a church member and then doing some food shopping for myself. I know I'll be getting to you tomorrow, reporting on Calvin's visit here. Stay tuned … you won't want to miss that!

David Lecternmann

• • •

From: Roz
Sent: Sunday, April 14, 2019 at 10:36 PM
To: RALPH
Subject: Gibberish to Entertain You!

Dear David Lecternmann aka Speaker of the House,
With a little bit of luck, I will attempt to tell you the steps to take (in non techie talk) so you can tape programs you may want to watch at your leisure:

Step 1-Make friends with your television/cable remote (find "guide" on the left and find "red dot" on the right)

Step 2- press guide and scroll (pressing one of the four arrows around the OK button in the middle … up, down, backward or forward) to the PBS channel on GUIDE and scroll to the time Sunday or Tuesday 9pm and find "Les Misérables "listed. I think there are 6 episodes beginning tonight.

Step 3- when you find the program and the time on GUIDE press the "red dot" that will say RECORD on the screen. If you have an option to press "record all episodes" press the OK button in the middle … it may ask aka "prompt" you to "confirm" which you will do by pressing the OK button again.

Step 4- voila, with a bit of luck you have recorded the program you wish to view "whenever"!

Step 5- when you are ready to watch the taped program you will need to press the button above the scroll arrows that reads: XFINITY.

Step 6- once you press XFINITY you will have a choice of headings that read "recordings", "saved". Scroll to "recording" or "saved" and scroll the down arrow to the program title and press OK and it should play your taped episode.

IF THIS DOES NOT WORK, immediately turn off the television and wait until Mori comes to visit and ask him to help you or call me, and I can try to walk you through the steps ... or ... WAIT UNTIL YOU ARE HERE AND I WILL WALK YOU THROUGH THE STEPS in person ...

Whew! I know this may be above my pay grade aka skill ... but once you master this you will be very pleased with the selected programs you have customized to your liking and the convenience of viewing times of your choice.

Yours truly,
The Non Geek Squad
Or the Non Nerd who pretends to be a Nerd Techie to impress someone who could totally care less about this activity!!
10-4 Over and Out

Sent from my iPhone

From: RALPH
Sent: Monday, April 15, 2019 at 11:32 AM
To: Roz
Subject: Re: Gibberish to Entertain You!

Good morning, Presch,
Confirming that I received your instructions about taping programs. Thanks be to thee (that's a carry-over from my Palm Sunday worship) for that, though I have not yet tried to set up the player. That's my challenge for Tuesday, before the PBS show repeats.

There was an email from Mori this morning extolling the pleasures of the place where they're staying. I want to give you a glimpse of what it's like. Those two pics reveal the natural and man-made features where they are. Wild sky, huh?

I awakened this morning to rain and intermittent lightning flashes, disappointed for the Marathon runners. However, about 8:30 the rain stopped, and the sun came out, giving us a beautiful day so far. I'm grateful for their comfort and safety as they strive for the finish line.

Otherwise, nothing new to report. Haven't heard from Calvin yet, which is OK. I have enough other things to consume my time.

Will be back to you later.
Patriot

● ● ●

From: RALPH
Sent: Monday, April 15, 2019 at 1:28 PM
To: Roz
Subject: My thoughts

Spiritual Match by RHI

Who withdrew you
Out of Xanadu,
And placed you there on my path?
Now, pleasing you;
A dream come true.
Surely we're in Eden at last.

Out of the blue
I'll soon be with you ...
A week that will pass in a flash.

Fresh like the dew,
Imagine love anew
With two persons sharing that path.

From: Roz
Sent: Monday, April 15, 2019 at 4:37 PM
To: RALPH
Subject: Your Thoughts ... My Response ... Breathless, beyond beyond

Don't ask how ...
Don't ask why ...

The now we embrace is brimming with beautiful, heartfelt romance and joy...

Two hearts that beat in sync ... a rhythm unique to Us.

Sent from my iPhone

• • •

From: RALPH
Sent: Tuesday, April 16, 2019 at 8:30 AM
To: Roz
Subject: Photo circa 1963

That's a lovely picture of you. Nice you found it readily ... sometimes it takes me days to find what I'm looking for. It's remarkable how parallel our lives progressed. It was just a year later that my wife and I married.

Your picture tells it all ... It's obvious why your husband chose you.

From: RALPH
Sent: Friday, April 19, 2019 at 9:31 PM
To: Roz
Subject: Spring Blossoms

Are you back in the quiet of your home now? Me too!

Our worship service was truly moving and closed with the ceremonial Holy Communion. For Christians the end of the Passion is tantamount to VICTORY! We entered the sanctuary in sadness ... we departed in joy.

Today we had 74 degrees, and the flowers are lovely. I'm going to try to send a couple of pictures. If I can't get them both on here, I'll send again. Then I will call you.

New Dell Owner

• • •

From: RALPH
Sent: Monday, April 22, 2019 at 9:16 AM
To: Roz
Subject: New evidence

Happy day-after,
Just want to show you that Spring is truly here.

After a quick breakfast I stepped out to the deck for a breath of fresh air
and found this. Apparently while I was away yesterday some friendly fowl
thought the protection under my roof would be a good place to set up "nest-
keeping"! The attached was assembled on top of the deck light fixture.

Looking out across the yard, there were two robins eyeballing me. As
calmly as possible I moved back into the house, to watch from within.
Now I shall have to avoid using the back door for a while.

Seeing this does put me in mind of my own impulses! Isn't life great?

From: Roz
Sent: Monday, April 22, 2019 at 12:06 PM
To: RALPH
Subject: Re: New evidence

Spring has sprung!!! New birth, rebirth, date of birth, birthing
new ideas!!!

This nest building has chosen a prestige Cambridge address and looks
to be a spacious construction ... may even be a duplex in design ... YEAH
IMPULSES! Life and nature, absolutely Great!

Sent from my iPhone

From: RALPH
Sent: Monday, April 22, 2019 at 3:39 PM
To: Roz
Subject: Re: New evidence

Hello Roz,
Enjoyed your upbeat reply to my note and photo, regardless of it being
"for the birds"!

I thought it may be a distraction from the deeper emotions you're feeling today. From all you've shared with me about your husband, I realize how strong the bond between the two of you was. So, on a date like today I know you can't get past reflecting on that relationship. It's unforgettable! I simply want you to know my empathy for you now. I'm with you in spirit and hoping your love of him and connection with me will give you peace and hope for the life ahead.

My love to you Roz.
Ralph

● ● ●

From: RALPH
Sent: Saturday, May 4, 2019 at 11:03 PM
To: Roz
Subject: Re: Touching message

To remember a loved one who made our lives richer for being a cherished part of our life, I've come to know the deep well of love that you are. You have been giving your love so generously to so many, and now it is I receiving an abundance of it. I'm learning to emulate you in many ways, but how can I ever have a capacity of love in my heart to match yours? With the measure of love I have for you I hope you'll not be disappointed!

● ● ●

From: RALPH
Sent: Monday, May 6, 2019 at 11:22 AM
To: Roz
Subject: Re: Roz and friend at the Green Market

We are melting in 90 degree temp! Blueberry scones and Baltimore Crab Cakes priority purchases! Thinking of US a week ago at this very scene!

Hi ... how is Monday going? I'm having a slow start! But the pic you sent was a perfect opener. The two of you seem made for each other.

There's a kind of easy-going style for both of you, great smiles, and I like the image of breezy hair. It looks like both of you were enjoying the market.

Saturday, I went to market also. I found some strawberries that were amazing, all oversized and tastefully ripe, so, so, good. I'll try to send you a pic. (Ha Ha, that'll be the day!) So much for now. Hoping the good times continue for you two. Stay cool!

• • •

From: RALPH
Sent: Tuesday, May 7, 2019 at 9:04 PM
To: Roz
Subject: The rhodies are blooming

A simple attachment to show you how 75 degrees F has affected the flora in my garden ... ah Spring! Of course, I'm "in the pink"! Will talk to you shortly.

• • •

From: RALPH
Sent: Wednesday, May 8, 2019 at 1:09 PM
To: Roz
Subject: Re: Memory Keepers!

Hi Presch,
Mori came and got my computer working ... that's the old one. Feels good to be able to communicate again.

I told him about making a 5" x 7" for you of my photo. Also, I've requested he make a 5" x 7" for me of the photo of you and me in front of the Oldenburg sculpture. Looking at it he said the print at the size you sent was a small size and the resolution was not as good for reproducing as a larger size would be. He's asking if you could send the largest size available. I'm sure you know what he means ... when you want to send an image, they give you four choices for what size. He'll try to do it soon.

I'll talk with you tonight. Until then, thinking of you.

From: Roz
Sent: Wednesday, May 8, 2019 at 11:24 PM
To: RALPH
Subject: Good Night and Good Morning!

Loved listening to your voice message (when I got home at 10:30 tonight) and hearing about the key pushed unknowingly into computer no man's land prompting you on a techie journey, thanks to your neighbor's questionable guidance, to purchase a new computer that most surely would bring you into the modern age of computer buzz … and the beat goes on with a renewed old computer, lots of buckaroos saved and a happy time back with your old friend! Yay messaging and re-connectivity with friends and relatives! Sometimes there really is a surprising outcome to situations of "mystery" in the cyberspace of the unknown…

The Dance Theatre of Harlem was outstanding!!! The spectrum of dance from classical to modern choreography ,with extraordinary bodies interpreting music and movement was a wonderful treat of an evening! The sold out audience was thrilled to experience the joy of this accomplished company begun in the 1960's to establish an African American Ballet Corp for talented young dancers to have a place and an identity. Bravo!

Hope you had an interesting Bible Study Session tonight …

I will resend the picture although I have tried to get back to the "option stage" to select a larger resolution but have not been successful in finding this step that presented itself at the first "send" last week when I forwarded the picture to you. Know this is disappointing for you … Mori is certainly welcome to try my phone and iPad … perhaps a new picture for enlargement in the future will please you since this one may not be retrievable??

I will be thinking of you tomorrow (or today as you will be reading this on Thursday, May 9th) … I know you will focus on the joys and special memories you cherish … and celebrate the day with love.

Sending My Best Hugs to You,
Roz

Sent from my iPad

From: RALPH
Sent: Thursday, May 9, 2019 at 10:58 AM
To: Roz
Subject: Re: Good Night and Good Morning!

Dear Roz,
You continue to delight me with your encouraging responses to my notes or phone calls to you. Your messages never leave me wanting ... you always feed my soul.

I was tired and discombobulated when I called last night and felt afterward that I wasn't very coherent explaining my condition at the end of the day. Yet this morning I found your upbeat, understanding, happy response. You're really such a treasure to me.

Mori's breathing new life into my old Dell truly was an exuberance. I'm going to rename my computer "Phoenix". It seems to be responding even better now than its performance before the problem. I will return the new components I bought, in accord with Dell's policy if I change my mind within 30 days. And yes, you're correct, I will save those "buckaroos".

Your response to the Harlem Dance Theatre performance was music to my ears! Sounds like it was an all-inclusive set of diverse choreography, leaving you begging for more as the program progressed. Your comment about the extraordinary bodies in movement brings to mind those sequences where they are wearing body-form tights which reveal all the beauty of the human body.

As you watched, you may have recalled my telling you about Mori shepherding minority high school students in Philadelphia to such performances, to give them awareness and encouragement regarding their career potential in the performing arts.

The Bible study last night was insightful, a good discussion about addressing person to person resolution of disagreement, especially when it wells up between members of the church family. (Does that bring to mind the issues related to the lectern)?

Your recognition of the significance of May 9 to my family, and the personal feelings you expressed for us is one more reason I have such deep love for you. Just as "she" remains with us, so you will be with me today as well. You are precious!

You are the wind beneath my wings

• • •

From: RALPH
Sent: Thursday, May 9, 2019 at 5:05 PM
To: Roz
Subject: Re: To make you SMILE!

You would really make me SMILE if I were next to you in that picture! However, I'll settle for your positivity and hugs.

• • •

From: Roz
Sent: Thursday, May 9, 2019 at 11:17 PM
To: RALPH
Subject: Date of Arrival Determined

Dear "Phoenix",
Please advise your renowned, and extraordinary articulator of expressively heartfelt emails aka owner and longtime friend that a Jet Blue ticket has been purchased for my for arrival at Logan June 7, 2019 at 4:31 pm! Once entered on the calendar, "happenings" can be planned and itineraries made. Happy Days ahead!

Yours truly,
Your Most Over the Moon Recipient of "Phoenix" missives!
Presch

Sent from my iPad

From: RALPH
Sent: Friday, May 10, 2019 at 7:17 AM
To: Roz
Subject: Re: Date of Arrival Determined

Dear Moonbeam,
Well Phoenix is certainly on top of things this morning! It brought the morning news, and the report is superb! Let the scheduling begin!

Your first-week-in-June arrival is earlier than expected ... "the more to share with you, my dear" said the wolf! That's less than a month away. Does life get any better?

I'm just grooming myself to get going for breakfast with my "rabbi", but first checked my Dell friend, and glad I did. The sun isn't up yet but your moonglow is already making this a splendid day. Thanks for being such a banner planner. Will be talking with you again at the other end of this day.

Your Welcoming Guy

• • •

From: RALPH
Sent: Sunday, May 12, 2019 at 8:34 AM
To: Roz
Subject: Re: Today is a good day for a good day!

Ah, Presch ... you look so fresh!

Such an early riser, again you're leading while I follow. You were up and active while I was still between the sheets (albeit calm in meditation). Today most surely is a good day, and I'm feeling it already in the wake of your note and the strength in your image. By all the simple treats you embody, I know I'm in your heart.

"I see clouds of blue and clouds of white. The bright blessed day, the dark sacred night. And I think to myself ... what a wonderful world" ! *

*Because you're part of it.

RHI

From: Roz
Sent: Tuesday, May 14, 2019 at 2:06 PM
To: RALPH
Subject: Research Break to share option ...

Shhh ... can only whisper since I am in "research mode". Thinking about the tentative road trip (possible departure early 7/18) to Indiana it occurred to me to check a destination three quarters of the drive west ... Cleveland is estimated to be 9 hours and 39 minutes from Boston (leaving 5 hours and 48 minutes of driving time to Bloomington).

We could do "a drive about `for old times' sake" if you wish before departing for Bloomington and perhaps make the Friday night "GREASE" performance ... and/ or spend more time on our return drive through Cleveland ...

Also requiring brain activity is the daunting challenge of packing aka clothing selections for an anticipated 3 month sojourn given weather dynamics in New England ... baffling to be sure. Promise not to bore you with this ... adapting Scarlett's approach to "think about this tomorrow" ... . and tomorrow and tomorrow, thank you Will!

Best impromptu plan ... eat chocolate (need energy)! Back to "the stacks" ...

Hope you are having success with your "projects".

Sent from my iPad

From: RALPH
Sent: Tuesday, May 14, 2019 at 6:22 PM
To: Roz
Subject: Re: Research Break to share option ...

Your shift to travel "research" came up with a brainstorm. Making Cleveland a part-way destination seems to me to be a good strategy for comfortable driving segments. I only wish I had some former "dear friends" living there, to welcome us into their home for a night ... a la your dear friend. I do have such a couple in the Columbus area, retired there on a small acreage, but the house condition leaves much to be desired.

My wife was always uncomfortable there (too much like roughing it) and I can't put you in that situation.

We can talk more about Cleveland tonight when I call you. I'm about ready to go the Men's Discussion Group tonight … 7 to 8 … I should be home before 9 pm.

Regarding your packing dilemma, for that length of time I think you need to take a 3-season wardrobe! Your Scarlett quote "think about this tomorrow" takes me back to Bill Clinton as well … "can't stop thinking about tomorrow"! Duh! Gotta get out of here now. Back to you shortly via wire.

• • •

From: RALPH
Sent: Thursday, May 16, 2019 at 8:32 AM
To: Roz
Subject: Re: I Love Lily of the Valley in the garden, in a bouquet, in a vase and as a Valentine!

I love that graphic image for a valentine … ! love the recipient much more! I hope the message penned inside expressed amply enough the abundant love I hold for you in my heart. Sweet morning to you.

The other R

• • •

From: Roz
Sent: Thursday, May 16, 2019 at 08:43 AM
To: RALPH
Subject: "Come From Away"

Just purchased tickets for your 1st Broadway Theatre Experience with LUCKY ME!!!

We have seats for the Sunday, August 4th Matinee at 3 pm at the Gerald Schoenfeld Theatre on W 45th Street (heart of the Theatre District)! I am so excited for us!

Sent from my iPhone

From: RALPH
Sent: Thursday, May 16, 2019 at 9:45 AM
To: Roz
Subject: Re: "Come From Away"

That's great news. You are fantastic at getting things done. I've never attended any shows in the Theater district so it will be a first for me. Exciting for me too. Thanks for moving ahead with the ticketing to assure seating for us. Will talk more about that later.

Delighted

• • •

From: RALPH
Sent: Friday, May 24, 2019 at 3:55 PM
To: Roz
Subject: Frame fame

Finally did the window sash,
Painted yesterday, what a bash!
Couldn't do it in a flash ...
Took a while but I saved some cash.
Forgive me 'cause this may seem brash,
But this's all for now ... I gotta dash!
Hittin' the shower ... splash!

• • •

From: RALPH
Sent: Monday, May 27, 2019 at 9:42 PM
To: Roz
Subject: Iris has opened

This little iris garden has been "the object of my affection" the past couple days. As more buds open, I'll send pics to you. Now (with eyes half closed) I'm heading to bed (and certain I'll have pleasant dreamzzzzzzzz).

From the Garden of the Finzi-Continis

• • •

From: Roz
Sent: Monday, May 27, 2019 at 9:57 PM
To: RALPH
Subject: Your Garden

Oh, how beautiful does your garden grow! Your loving care and eye
for natural beauty makes your garden a luscious feast for the observer
to behold and rapturous for one's spirit. Although I have only seen
suggestions from a window or a captured photograph, I am certain my
imagination does not do your's and mother nature's visuals the justice
each tenderly nurtured flowerbed or carefully trimmed bush deserves.
I do look forward to personally viewing the Gardens of the Insinger's
Fingers in the very near future!

Thank you for the Purple Iris to dream me to sleep!
Sigh

Sent from my iPhone

From: RALPH
Sent: Tuesday, May 28, 2019 at 7:27 AM
To: Roz
Subject: re: Your Garden

Hello night visitor,
How sweet of you late last night, to reply to my garden pictures. I hope
you did have dreams of irises … regal purple suits you. As for me, I slid
between the sheets, and that's the last thing I remember. I slept soundly!

I loved your poetic reference to the Gardens of Insinger's Fingers. That's
your imaginative touch again. Now I'm encouraged to do mora, with my
flora … perhaps a mini-Versailles before your imminent arrival.

It's a beautiful morning here. Due to the extensive rest, I had, I was up early.
As for you, I hope you are still deep in Dreamland, with every vision rapturous!

Wishing you a great day, excited for you to come and "make MY day".

Aiming for Eden

Sent from my iPhone

From: Roz
Sent: Tuesday, May 28, 2019 at 7:45am
To: Ralph
Subject: Re: Your garden

Dear "Clint",
It is my plan/hope as your "genie" to make your wish(es) come true in less than two weeks!

YOU create the best response(s) in me from smiles to giggles to deep pleasurable sighs ... thank you for You!

Eve

Sent from my iPhone

• • •

From: Roz
Sent: Thursday, May 30, 2019 at 9:54 AM
To: RALPH
Subject: Being a "Squirrel" has benefits ...

Good Thursday Morning,
Sitting at my desk this morning organizing stuff for my departure next Friday (in one week), I shuffled into a folder that has stopped my progress and afforded me beautiful reflective moments!

I found the first emails we exchanged that I had printed "just because" ... August 14, 2018, was the date of our meeting at the MFA ... you, in your very thoughtful way, had emailed Karen a "thank you" for the "artful prelude" to our threesome lunch and the ensuing conversation. You mentioned your pleasure at meeting Karen's mother and Karen mentioned the email to me. Nice ...

I asked for your email to "thank you for the meeting" and to wish you happy trails as you had mentioned your upcoming nostalgic road trip ... AND THE REST IS HISTORY ...

I am overwhelmed with the power of destiny or the "spiritual choreographed script" that has brought us to this extraordinary moment in time. How lucky we are to have been given the gift of our connection/ friendship/relationship!!!!

Joyfully Yours

Sent from my iPhone

From: RALPH
Sent: Thursday, May 30, 2019 at 3:29 PM
To: Roz
Subject: Re: Being a "Squirrel" has benefits …

Yes, nature teaches us many things, including "squirreling away" items that will have significant importance later. And I might add, grant us a second serving of pleasure! Your reflective moments have been on my mind during the hours since I viewed and re-viewed your comments. You wrote in such a loving manner, as if a found walnut broken open presented you with a golden kernel. I'm truly moved how you embrace our relationship, as I do too. It began as a friendship, advanced into a relationship, and now I am captivated with "connection" to you.

I've been consuming time trying to complete some tasks before I depart for Brookline. That done, I'm ready to collect my things and head out of here, but first I had to respond to your writing. It is beautiful, and I know it will keep my mind occupied into the night, certainly as I slip into bed. Like you I believe our lives have been choreographed by a loving Power, and we are blessed.

Squirrel 2

• • •

From: RALPH
Sent: Sunday, June 2, 2019 at 10:06 AM
To: Roz
Subject: Thanks

Good Sunday morning, Presch,
Taking a few minutes to pass on an email I received from my former pastor in Michigan, still a good friend.

I sent him a set of the drawings I did for my current church, to show him what we did here. I was quite certain he would like to look it over. I had done some design work for his church too. It was gratifying to hear his response, apparently he still feels good about what we did when I was a member of Holy Spirit Church there.

Great comment about my packaging, indicating my determination that nothing would crush my mailing!

The spirit of the Sabbath includes you.
Servant

From: Roz
Sent: Sunday, June 2, 2019 at 10:36 AM
To: RALPH
Subject: Re: Thanks

Thank you for sharing this message with me. So nice for you to know that your friend acknowledges and compliments your expertise/skills and reinforces for you the knowledge that you have created a warm and welcoming environment for your fellow church congregants ... to enjoy and feel spiritual strength.

Your gift of designing/structuring a domain that inspires must give you great pleasure.

Your Admirer

Sent from my iPhone

● ● ●

From: Roz
Sent: Tuesday, June 4, 2019 at 6:42 PM
To: RALPH
Subject: I agree with you that sometimes a cartoon can "nail it"!

From: RALPH
Sent: Tuesday, June 4, 2019 at 10:45 PM
To: Roz
Subject: Re: I agree with you that sometimes a cartoon can "nail it"!

Ah, yes! Peanuts was such a simple but insightful source of "fast food" style philosophy. Charles Schulz was so good at gathering bits of wit, humor, and heart, then passing it on to us through the lips of children. You described it perfectly ... how he so often "nailed it"!

• • •

From: Roz
Sent: Wednesday, June 5, 2019 at 10:47 PM
To: RALPH
Subject: Ludens Cherry Cough Drops (that can make your tongue reddish)!

Just emailing to say how much I love, love, love our conversations! "Topics galore, sentiments to share, fun happenings to recall and profound connectivity to explore ... all of this and more filled with laughter and joy!"

Once we say "goodnight", smiling is my lasting expression ... an exercise that lines my lips and face with the absolute best feeling!

I am so happy having shared our hour conversation ... perfect ending to this difficult day ... THANK YOU!

Please be gentle with your nose ... cause your nose knows!
Presch

Sent from my iPhone

From: RALPH
Sent: Thursday, June 6, 2019 at 7:33 AM
To: Roz
Subject: Re: Ludens Cherry Cough Drops (that can make your tongue reddish)!

Good morning Presch,
Last night as I finished prepping for bed, I took a last look at the inbox and found your perfectly expressed commentary of our nightly monopoly of the phone line between our two dwellings. The potpourri of topics and the ease with which we move from one to another, is laughable. But the magic in all of it is how it becomes balm for a somewhat trying day. I conclude the session with a more positive state of mind, thanks to your insights.

The nose knows,
I still treasure my nose-blows,
What will I do if the nose goes,
And through the gap my throat shows?

Sorry, let's get more serious!

Hand the words gently around and unclose them from your protective heart. Go ahead and speak.

Honor this beautiful life now curling in on itself folding over its charmed spark and rounding down into deep silence. one final stone.

Presch, I love you all the more for your contributions to others around you. Now I have to go. Much to do today. But you'll never be absent from my thoughts.

Ralph

• • •

From: Roz
Sent: Tuesday, June 10, 2019 at 9:38 PM
To: RALPH
Subject: Home safely!!

Dearest You,
Hoping your return drive was easy and smooth! Thank you for today and taking care of me getting to my friend and my next stop on my enviable travels ...

Wishing the sweetest of dreams with love,
Presch

Sent from my iPhone

From: RALPH
Sent: Tuesday, June 11, 2019 at 12:25 PM
To: Roz
Subject: Re: Home safely!!

Hellooooooo! Writing primarily to acknowledge receiving your message last night, written before I called you. Just as you were thinking of me, my mind was full of you.

The drive home was easy, because I discarded the iPhone directions, and followed your "post it" note of the streets to take. The roads were empty compared to our drive down to Needham. It was a perfect time to review our day.

Driving home, the only troubling moment was on 1-95 near Lincoln, when some unrelenting driver in the second lane was coming up aside of where I was in the first lane, he wanting off at the next exit (apparently) and unwilling to slow down and get behind me to make his exit. So, he chose to attempt pulling in front of me instead. I leaned on the horn {that I was right at his side) while he kept crowding toward me and me moving toward the shoulder. With my horn still blaring at his side, I put the pedal to the metal and surged ahead of him and got out of the squeeze. There are so many jerks like that on the expressways, who just can't/won't choose the safe way of getting behind someone to exit ... their pride will be destroyed if they don't assert themselves and get in front of you. Oh well, my angels continued with me the rest of the way, for a peaceful return to my house.

Earlier today we were engaged in some significant discussion about how our relationship continues. I think both of us revealed our personal concerns about specific issues, which I hope each of us can ponder as we proceed with sharing other activities we favor. Let our hearts guide us regarding those other "personal concerns".

Now enjoy your overnight stay with your friend. You have other matters to consider. Know that OUR time will come again soon.

Driver

• • •

From: Roz
Sent: Friday, August 9, 2019 at 9:00 PM
To: RALPH
Subject: Wonder what creative expression Leonard Cohen would pen of this pose of the two of Us at The Jewish Museum in NYC? 8/6/2019

Sent from my iPhone

From: RALPH
Sent: Saturday, August 10, 2019 at 9:44 AM
To: Roz
Subject: Re: Wonder what creative expression Leonard Cohen would pen of this pose of the two of Us at The Jewish Museum in NYC? 8/6/2019

Good morning,
How sweet it was to find you in this morning's inbox. The night was lonely but now you've brought me close to you and warmed my spirit again.

That photo comes back readily ... it was a happy moment, which makes me disappointed now seeing me with such a dour look on my face! I wish my expression was more indicative of the pleasure I had visiting the museum with you, observing the collection of Jewish art exhibited there.

I've got to get on with things now ... this and that in preparation for the weekend activities. I hope you continue feeling better, that the medication is working. I'll be back to you again toward the end of the day. Lord, let it be a good one!

OY guy

· · ·

From: Roz
Sent: Sunday, August 11, 2019 at 2:09 PM
To: RALPH
Subject: Special Request!

Greetings from the Tuscan Kitchen Marketplace in Salem NH (after grandson's winning baseball game)!

Purchasing some freshly prepared Italian foodstuffs for us to sample during the week that will require coldness so please bring your cooler tomorrow night (with ice packets) to keep foodstuffs refrigerated while we have dinner! These tasty items come personally recommended ...

Thank you!!
Ciao

Sent from my iPhone

From: RALPH
Sent: Monday, August 12, 2019 at 8:10 AM
To: Roz
Subject: Re: Special Request!

The cooler is ready to go, wanting to play its part in our survival! Personally, I am having a hard time waiting, to sample some of those choice items you've selected. I'll be watching the hands on the clock all through the day. Hurry evening! See you soon.

Professional Taster

· · ·

From: RALPH
Sent: Monday, August 26, 2019 at 7:17 PM
To: Roz
Subject: "Once" aka "ice" …

Hellooooooo! I was so involved running about town during that time that I didn't catch up to you until now. I hope my lack of response didn't curb your enthusiasm.

My morning went slowly, quietly drinking hot Arnold P's and hot coffee for breakfast, along with fruits and a piece of toast. Afterward I was coughing a lot and not feeling great, so I chose to lie down again and rest. Somewhat better later, I decided I better get going before the day dissolved and I had nothing to show for it.

About 11 a.m. I gassed up the car, then moved on to the City Services office to get a fresh supply of those green compostable trash bags (free replacements by the way). Returned home for a quick chicken salad sandwich (thanks to you) and then took off again for the car wash. I don't know what those little droplets on the car were, but they were oily and I wanted to eliminate any possibility of them getting "burned" onto the car finish.

It was nearly time for my doctor appointment, so I headed there, having a few minutes to spare. That procedure went easily enough … an injection into the palm of my hand, centered up under the bottom of my middle finger. It's already feeling better. The doc said after three injections, if that doesn't eliminate the finger locking up, it's time to have the surgical procedure. It's a small cut in the palm to get to a tendon or something, then a few absorbent stitches and it's done. He says I could be using the hand later that day. Sounds simple, but you know what Mr. Murphy says! Following that I returned home and took a nap which left me feeling better.

Checking emails I found yours, along with some exceptional pics. A couple take-away thoughts for me to heed: don't wear short shorts and don't wear snow-white shorts! They don't suit me. I did like the one at the table, eating the lobster roll. It looked like "Having lunch with Carl Sandburg."

I delighted in hearing from you, to know you were thinking about me. I'm not in great voice now, but I will call you later.

From: Roz
Sent: Monday, August 26, 2019 at 7:55 PM
Subject: One of my Favorite NYC Moments! Who is taking the selfie? Team effort!

Sent from my iPhone

From: RALPH
Sent: Monday, August 26, 2019 at 8:08 PM
To: Roz
Subject: Re: One of my Favorite NYC Moments! Who is taking the selfie? Team effort!

I think you get credit for that snapshot. I like it ... you look great! We took a superb "bite" out of the Big Apple.

• • •

From: Roz
Sent: Wednesday, August 28, 2019 at 5:40 AM
To: RALPH
Subject: Good Morning!

Surprise! I am awake on "Ralph Time" not quite ready to start the day but thinking about YOU ... Wishing you a successful 1st day of your "rental project prep" ... as you prepare the scene for your next tenants you are the " man of many talents".

Smiles to You!

Sent from my iPhone

From: RALPH
Sent: Wednesday, August 28, 2019 at 7:19 AM
To: Roz
Subject: Re: Good Morning!

And a beautiful morning to you, my wake-up ANGEL. It must have been your spiritual presence, so early, setting the course of my day. My response is late because today I chose to return to my daily custom of first doing a morning devotion. When I'm alone that gives me comfort and direction. Now, finding your note, and your SMILES, has given impetus to my commitment to accomplish the work today.

I would like to write more, but I can't resist the force that is motivating me to "get moving"! Return to your sleep, and the serenity of a lovely DREAM.

As for me, I'm ...
On The Road Again

. . .

From: Roz
Sent: Wednesday, August 28, 2019 at 9:27 PM
To Ralph:
Subject: Our Plum Island Getaway!

Home away from "home" for the next couple of days. Friday will be devoted to the beach and the "seaside" or as the saying goes: "sea-ing is believing"! Smiling with YOU!

From: RALPH
Sent: Wednesday, August 28, 2019 at 10:34 PM
To: Roz
Subject: Re: Our Plum Island Getaway!

Well, such a cozy little cottage. You two must be enjoying the sojourn there. How far is it from the porch to the water? Keep your toes out of the water. Plum Island sharks love those red toenails. Be careful when on the porch too ... every so often people lounging out there have been attacked by a (use low, lyrical, muffled voice) "land shark"! Yikes! I'll check in with you in the morning ... if you've survived!

Captain Ahab

From: Roz
Sent: Wednesday, August 28, 2019 at 10:56 PM
To: RALPH
Subject: Re: Our Plum Island Getaway!

I am laughing myself to sleep!! Hehe haha! You are the "bestest
Captain" I know!!!!

Sent from my iPhone

From: RALPH
Sent: Thursday, August 29, 2019 at 8:14 AM
To: Roz
Subject: Re: Our Plum Island Getaway!

Hi Presch
Just writing to let you know I'm doing well this morning. Clear nose and
throat. About to go down for a bite to eat, then off to my INR check-up this
morning. I'll go down to the condo after that, to open up and see how
things turned out with the floor refinishing.

Had a good rain last night, beneficial to the hedge. This morning when I
looked out, I could see the black car was back in our neighbor's driveway.
Their waiter/employee must have returned it after closing the restaurant
last night.

I'm sure you and Karen have your own major plans for today. Safe travel to
you. I'll get back to you later.

Luvvvvvvvvvvvvvvvvvvvvvvv

• • •

From: Roz
Sent: Thursday, August 29, 2019 at 10:20 PM
To: RALPH
Subject: Wishing You Sweet Dreams

Just arrived at the cottage on Plum Island ... long day and very tired but
you remain a constant in my thoughts!

From: RALPH
Sent: Friday, August 30, 2019 at 7:05 AM
To: Roz
Subject: Re: Wishing You Sweet Dreams

You always have something cheery and enlightening to give me a lift. Speaking of "hope", I hope you slept well after your long day of circulating this metropolis. I'm feeling better after a good night's rest … just about to go down for a bit of breakfast. Then off to begin my marathon day of painting.

Mori and family are safely back home. He will be joining me today to do the upgrading of the apartment. Of course, we'll have lots to talk about as we work side by side.

May the Lord bless you as you proceed with your day. You are beautiful and I miss you.

No Michelangelo

From: Roz
Sent: Friday, August 30, 2019 at 9:24 PM
To: RALPH
Subject: Wishing You Sweet Dreams

"From One Adirondack to Another Adirondack" … how's the sitting?

• • •

From: RALPH
Sent: Friday, August 30, 2019, 10:07 PM
To: Roz
Subject: Re: Plum Island Getaway 8/30/2019

Oh what a lovely picture that is of you … did Karen snap that? And the seating is "maah-vellus!" You know that the name of the chair is graceless slang for "A dear on deck". I would welcome the opportunity to snuggle there with you and the hydrangeas!

• • •

From: Roz
Sent: Saturday, August 31, 2019 at 6:00 AM
To: RALPH
Subject: May "The Roll" Be With You!

Wishing you smooth and easy "paint rolls" today as you finalize your apartment prep for your new tenants tomorrow! Hoping your paint strokes will be easy and that you will take care of You as you accomplish your much anticipated goals.

We will be off to Chickapee, MA (half hour before Lenox-Tanglewood) later this morning to be in "picnic mode" on the lawn outside of the Koussevitzky Shed at 5pm to hear Trombone Shorty in Concert at 7pm! Then back to Chickapee (fun to type) for the night and back home tomorrow!

I am and will be thinking of You and your "awesomeness !!!

Sent from my iPhone

From: RALPH
Sent: Saturday, August 31, 2019 at 6:45 AM
To: Roz
Subject: Re: May "The Roll" Be With You!

Good morning, easy riser,
I'm up, truly up, and just about to enter the shower. But first I decided I better check my inbox, and of course, there you are. Such sweet encouragement to accomplish my job today!

Safe and happy travels to you, easy rider. I know it will be comfortable for you, sharing such good company. Pray that Tanglewood will captivate you ... no bugs to notice you and no notes to bug you!

I'm complimented by your closing comment because you are awesomeness personified.

Peter Fonda (R.I.P.)

* * *

From: Roz
Sent: Saturday, August 31, 2019 at 4:46 PM
To: RALPH
Subject: Here we are at Tanglewood 8/31/2019

We have claimed our lawn space to picnic before Trombone Shorty performs in the Shed at 7pm! The temperature is 70 degrees ... as the sun sets the temp will drop so we have blankets and shawls!

Hoping you are pleased with all you accomplished today and can take a deep sigh and rest now!

Missing You ...

From: RALPH
Sent: Sunday, September 1, 2019 at 5:05 PM
To: Roz
Subject: Re: Here we are at Tanglewood 8/31/2019

What a loving threesome in an awesome setting. I hope the program was equally impressive. Kudos to whoever managed the selfie. Oh that all we men might spend our leisure with such splendid companions.

I'm really glad you were able to get to Tanglewood. Was Trombone Shorty worth the trip? If nothing else you were in touch with the magnificence of the Berkshires! (Though I've seen more beautiful Tetons here in Cambridge).

My sort of leisure was two days of prep and paint! Hauling all my assorted gear and paint supplies to the South End was the first struggle. Then the painting nearly "threw me under the bus"! Thank the Lord for Mori ... he more than pulled his weight both days. Being able to work together, while able to talk too, kept me sane. (He was of course a Presch substitute, because that's what you always do for me). The final part that almost did me in was cleaning up and loading up all the stuff I'd hauled down there. It was late and dark, just 10 pm when I drove into the garage. I was exhausted and went right to bed. I woke up this morning, very tired but remembering how truly sharp the place looked from all we did.

Today is my Sabbath ... my day of rest, and I did. After the church service I came home, went out on the deck to the chaise and fell asleep .

I'm thinking of you always and missing you. I have a rather open week except for the landscape man who's coming to fertilize the hedge and check one of my trees Wednesday, and on Friday Calvin and I have been invited to a brunch. You could come back here Wed afternoon if you don't mind my taking off for that brunch Friday. Or you could come back Friday afternoon, and we'd have the weekend and continue into the next week(s). Think it over and let's talk about it this evening.

Having missed lunch, I'm going to get started with dinner shortly. Looking forward to talking with you, hearing about where you are and what's up tomorrow.

Thanks for the pics you sent. But it's just not the same as holding you close! Be talking with you soon ...

Tired Michelangelo

• • •

From: Roz
Sent: Monday, September 2, 2019 at 6:33 AM
To: RALPH
Subject: Good Labor Day Morning!

By all accounts, you have done your "laboring" ... so how will you spend today? Happy plans, I hope.

We will be at home ... I will be watching the weather channel and news as this frightening Hurricane Dorian heads east and north and comes ashore sometime today.

My friend has been sending constant updates.. She is hunkered down at home with friends who have come to her house since she has a generator.

This is a very scary disaster about to happen at winds of 185 mph and higher at last report. I am grateful that my condo is shuttered but am anxious for the disaster that awaits so many along the eastern coastline. My hopes and prayers are focused on all who are in the path of this devastating "natural" happening.

Thank you for being my positive and wondrous touchstone!

Sent from my iPhone

From: RALPH
Sent: Monday, September 2, 2019 at 8:01 AM
To: Roz
Subject: Re: Good Labor Day Morning!

Up and around here, not busily, just assessing my "home base" to settle on something I should do today.

Like you I'm caught up in the drama Dorian poses for YOUR home base, specifically your friends there. The power of such strong winds is horrifying. I've been in touch with my friend in Tallahassee. He has done what he can for protection and is prepared to hang in there. I'm so glad you are secure here in the comfort of Beantown now. It's not paradise but it is a refuge!

You've had your own whirlwind week so relax today. I will do a few simple tasks but nothing strenuous ... I'm still feeling the strain of condoitis! That lounge on the deck is looking more inviting every minute. Comfort+ tranquility+ dream=Roz!

Got to have a bite to eat and put Keurig through its paces. Back to you soon.

Carl
(No not Sandburg ... it's Carl Philipp Emanuel Bach ... I'm having great music with my coffee this morning.)

• • •

From: Roz
Sent: Saturday, September 14, 2019 at 6:08 PM
To: RALPH
Subject: Your Orchid Gift to Karen has a new home!

From: RALPH
Sent: Saturday, September 14, 2019 at 9:34 PM
To: Roz
Subject: Re: Your Orchid Gift to Karen has a new home!

So happy to see the orchid in such comfortable surroundings. Looks much better out-of-box and plastic wrapping! Thanks for the extra connection to me, with visual accompaniment too. Your email and phone chat make a lovely end to my day. I'll be dreaming of you … absent but warming my heart.

Lonely Boy

● ● ●

From: Roz
Sent: Monday, October 7, 2019 at 7:56 AM
To: RALPH
Subject: Thinking of You and wishing you Happy FAMILY Week!

Enjoy togetherness!

From: RALPH
Sent: Monday, October 7, 2019 at 10:21 AM
To: Roz
Subject: Re: Thinking of You and wishing you Happy FAMILY Week!

Wow! What a great introduction to the morning! You look fantastic and I wish I was there to embrace you. Wonderful results with the hair … ! love it.

Thinking of you. No distractions from the guests, who are on their way up the north coast all day today. I have some good hours to take care of personal business until they return sometime tonight.

Going out in a minute to do some banking and food acquisition, then back to work around the house. Thanks for the lift I got from your photo gift. Missing you!

Don Wan

From: Roz
Sent: Friday, October 11, 2019 at 2:00 PM
To: RALPH
Subject: As the autumn leaves are falling , trees are blossoming and flowers are blooming!

We are waiting for you!

From: RALPH
Sent: Friday, October 11, 2019 at 3:18 PM
To: Roz
Subject: Re: As the autumn leaves are falling , trees are blossoming and flowers are blooming!

What beautiful florals. You are living in Eden! That flowering tree is outstanding ... stealing the show! You can't imagine how much I look forward to being with you there.

• • •

From: Roz
Sent: Saturday, October 12, 2019 at 5:24 PM
To: RALPH
Subject: This was my afternoon!

You were with me for the 3.5 hours!

https://www.metopera.org/season/in-cinemas/2019-20-season/turandot-live-in-hd/#Videos

Sent from my iPhone

From: RALPH
Sent: Saturday, October 12, 2019 at 10:22 PM
To: Roz
Subject: Re: This was my afternoon!

What powerful means for me to end my day. The videos did play out on my computer, and it was exceptional. To see it on the big screen must have been captivating. I loved those brief sequences, regret not being there with you.

• • •

From: Roz
Sent: Wednesday, October 16, 2019 at 2:34 PM
To: RALPH
Subject: Keeping COOL thoughts of YOU

From: RALPH
Sent: Wednesday, October 16, 2019 at 3:03 PM
To: Roz
Subject: Re: Keeping COOL thoughts of YOU

With 93 F outside, 71 F in the car must have been chilling. I know someone hot to slip in next to you! I suppose the next best thing is to keep "groovin' while you're moovin'!"

While we're chatting music-wise, "Don't Stop Thinkin' About the Morrow"!

• • •

From: Roz
Sent: Friday, November 15, 2019 at 10:19 PM
To: RALPH
Subject: Yeah grandson/Mr Green

His high school performance in "CLUE" was fun and successful.

From: RALPH
Sent: Friday, November 15, 2019 at 11:47 PM
To: Roz
Subject: Re: Yeah grandson/Mr Green

There were some sweet moments for your grandson after the performance. He's looking fantastic and the rest of you too. Couldn't believe he's so tall. You are a tall woman, but next to him you're diminutive ... and delightful ... and de-lovely! You were radiant with pride..

I'll be waiting to hear from you tomorrow, as you shove off, or en route, or when you are back home. Safe travels to you.

• • •

From: RALPH
Sent: Sunday, November 17, 2019 at 7:01 AM
To: Roz
Subject: Re: 108 is a WOW! I am thrilled!!!

Dear Presch,
What a pleasure to find your super-positive response to the improvements you made in your home. I know it must have been on your mind constantly while you were away. Now you can put your mind to rest … you have made it YOUR home. From the pictures it does look much more refined, sensitively improved by the changes you made. I am excited now to see it myself.

I'm up early to prepare a pie for the November church dinner today. I'll take a Dutch Apple pie. The theme of the meal is "international" … bring something related to your cultural history. I think the nationality is "Deutsch" but people over the years couldn't manage that and deflated it to Dutch!

So, I've got to get cooking. Will call you later, probably this afternoon. Now that you are up, savor the fresh character of your home. Then prepare to come and see another "character" in his home. Can't wait!

Warm Heart

• • •

From: Mori
Sent: Thursday, November 28, 2019 at 1:50 AM
To: ROZ & RALPH
Subject: Mark's Sketchbook 11/27/2019

Great to see you both tonight! And thanks for coming over and sharing items from the sketchbook. Was very interesting talking with you both, especially about having guests!

Roz, have a great Thanksgiving with your family, and I'm sorry I won't see you on Sat afternoon and that we can't all be together Sat night but hope you all have a fun time.

Look forward to our next time together, and thank you again for the quiche, the NOLA inspired food we will make, and the cookies for the girls. Very thoughtful of you!

Love to you both, and Happy Thanksgiving officially now!
Mori

• • •

From: Mori
Sent: Monday, December 2, 2019 at 3:20 AM
To: ROZ & RALPH
Subject: Re: A Shared I-Pad Moment! 11/30/2019

Thanks Roz for sharing these cute photos!, And thanks again to both of you for spending time with my daughter on Saturday.

Thanks also for your help trying to find that lost mitten, and as you've heard it turned up in the bottom of one of the bags earlier today, but we really appreciated your concern and help.

Roz, I believe you are leaving Tuesday or maybe Wednesday, and I know I won't see you and we may not even be in touch. But I wanted to say again how nice it was to see you and we already look forward to your next visit and having a little more time. I'm sorry you won't be here later this month because I will finally have a little break in my schedule with a few open days here and there and that will make a big difference. But safe travels and enjoy the rest of the holiday season and will keep in touch and see you the next time you're back in town.

And thanks again also for the treats and food for all of us that you brought over. Really helpful and appreciated!

With best wishes to you both,
Mori

• • •

From: RALPH
Sent: Wednesday, December 4, 2019 at 6:44 PM
To: Karen
Subject: Remembering last Saturday evening

Hi Karen,
In all likelihood you've heard that Roz is home again. She texted (?) me from the PBI baggage claim about 4:45 p.m. so apparently, she departed Logan on time and landed on time.

We were delighted to have so many days to be together, and I'm grateful to you for your kind understanding of what that meant to me. Nevertheless, I did feel a bit selfish in taking her away from your family activities during the holiday weekend.

Both Roz and I were pleased to have you come for dinner with us that Saturday evening. Aside from enjoying your company, it gave us the opportunity to see how well we can work together putting a dinner together. We expect to do more of that.

You have our thanks for the impressive gift you brought. The FireStick itself is a generous gift, but beyond that was the expertise and time you gave to get it up and running for our pleasure. We did use it each evening after, Roz knowing how, and educating me as well. I think we are both "certified" now. :-)

Your friendship means a great deal to me, including your extended family. I've appreciated the invitations to join you for various events over the past summer, and I hope for more such occasions to be with you as we move into a new year.

Thanks again.
With sincere regard,
Ralph

• • •

From: Roz
Sent: Saturday, December 7, 2019 at 1:06 PM
To: Ralph
Subject: Constancy is warmth from Me to YOU!

Off to purchase Holiday Gifts! Thinking of YOU! :)

From: RALPH
Sent: Saturday, December 7, 2019, 3:22 PM
To: Roz
Subject: Re: Constancy is warmth from Me to YOU!

Certainly an outstanding day down there and a beautiful environment. Perfect for your shopping pleasure. Can imagine you concentrating on finding just the right thing for each loved one … especially the grandchildren. You are truly the gift that keeps on giving!

Your comment "Off to purchase Holiday Gifts! Thinking of YOU!" evokes my anticipation. I hope thinking of me means a lift in your spirit, not a gift on your list. As you must be aware, being with you is the one and only gift I desire. It's the personal warmth from you to me.

Hoping you have a successful day concluding your gift purchases.

Now here is all I have for you today … but it runs deeeeeep.

From: Roz
Sent: Sunday, December 8, 2019 at 10:02
To: Ralph
Subject: Constancy is warmth from Me to YOU!

"Making sure this picture is perfectly straight! Did it"!!!

• • •

From: RALPH
Sent: Monday, December 9, 2019 at 8:25 AM
To: Roz
Subject: Re: Soon to be Very Familiar Surroundings!

Oh yes, familiar and heartwarming, it can't come soon enough.

The photos are wonderful. ..I'm making you my official personal photographer. You caught the "Z" pose perfectly. I wasn't aware that you were snapping that, but you surely caught me in an intense moment. I expect there will be more of that when I'm with you soon. Let the excitement begin!

• • •

From: Roz
Sent: Wednesday, December 18, 2019 at 3:20 PM
To: Ralph
Subject: On the Kitchen Table in front of Ralph's Chair! Eleven days and counting ...

From: RALPH
Sent: Wednesday, December 18, 2019 at 11:47 PM
To: Roz
Subject: Re: On the Kitchen Table in front of Ralph's Chair! Eleven days and counting ...

That is a beautiful Christmas Cactus ... keep that blooming for my arrival. Loved the chat with you tonight ... bless you for calling.
Now to bed ...

A "CLOSING""
IS IN ORDER ...

Dear Reader,

Now it is time to end our email story. As you may have noticed, much of our communication these last few months focused on long and insightful phone conversations that strengthened our connectivity and enriched our shared feelings. Those lengthy and detailed emails that helped us "get to know one another" fast became history.

We have reached a time in our relationship that makes spending time together a priority. Appreciating the old saying, we aren't getting any younger, we offer now our Beyond Beyond closing thoughts.

With a turn of the page ...

R&R

Roz's Epilogue

As I reflect on the years and months of our emails, I know that Ralph and I realized after a few months that there was so much more to our growing relationship than being "email pen pals". It was so easy to share our thoughts and feelings ... there was a sense of trust and respect permeating our expressions ... although humor and wit played a strong role in our writings, there was always an unspoken depth and substance to our messages. We had serious, heartfelt exchanges (written and phoned) about our backgrounds, our marriages of many years, our families, our life goals, our spiritual strengths, our travels of enrichment, our cultural interests, the importance of music and art in our lives, our regrets and our successes ... the more we opened ourselves to each other the more we yearned to know if what we were feeling was real.

We realized our communications were energizing us... each day we looked forward to "talking" by email or by phone ... we sensed a feeling of vitality and renewal ... could we be reliving our youthful wishes and desires? We recognized how significant just being together in "silence" miles apart was bonding us. We grew comfortable with our similarities and our differences ... at this stage of our lives there was no reason to be anything other than ourselves. We loved telling each other stories about experiences and friends of our past ... we met each other's current and long standing friends (some in person and some electronically and felt instant connectivity).

We never tire of learning and observing each other's talents and skills ... we welcome each new day with joy and renewal and end each day with deep feelings of shared fulfillment and contentment.

We could continue our "story" regaling you with road trips, learning extraordinary coincidences, touring new places and experiencing new tastes, repeating over and over again to each other how lucky we are ... how wondrous is this gift of each other to each other ... we are so fortunate ... we are so grateful.

We know in our hearts that we are meant to be together ... to blend our separate lives together making us a couple who measure our living moments as "our moments" in this last beautiful chapter of our lives.

Ralph's Epilogue

What Roz and I have experienced the past few years is now history. It began casually as a hope for friendship ... it has blended into a sincere and lasting love.

Sometime after first getting acquainted I invited Roz to have dinner with me. That evening kindled an unusual mutual interest in both of us. It seemed we had much to share! Months of emails followed. We realized we had discovered a level of understanding and common personal values that inspired us to choose a new direction in our lives. We were offered an open-ended ticket somewhere and felt challenged to pursue the opportunities together. Where might our choices take us?

During the months of communicating, we found a common bond in wit and humor. The question though, was how do we respond to more serious issues like compatibility within our families, or our willingness to accept each other's established social relationships? What were the personal interests and spiritual priorities to keep us excited, and driven to explore more in the years ahead?

Our correspondence had revealed an attitude of agreeability between us, but how flexible might we be for compromising or adjusting to more serious issues that might arise in a relationship?

Despite our advanced years, we found some evidence of a young-at-heart attitude. Could we proceed confidently into a new shared life that would be viable and even thrive?

We believed our depth of love and the trust we had in one another was strong enough to dispel any uncertainty. Instead, it would bring new love and happiness to both of us in our remaining years. With that belief firm in our minds, we chose to become partners for life.

Roz Lewy is a retired high school teacher and former chocolatier. She was a reader for print handicapped audiences in New Orleans and Washington, D.C. Roz has a daughter, a son and four grandchildren. This is her first book. Roz spends her summers in Cambridge, Massachusetts, and winters in Palm Beach Gardens, Florida, with charming Ralph.

Ralph Insinger, a retired architect, has a son and two granddaughters. He grew up in a rural environment in central Missouri, proceeding then to college for architecture studies, that later afforded him the opportunity to become one of the architectural designers of the World Trade Center towers in New York City. *Beyond Beyond* is his first experience writing a book. Between designing a building or writing a book, he is uncertain which is more formidable. Ralph spends summers in Cambridge, Massachusetts, and winters in Palm Beach Gardens, Florida, with the extraordinary Roz.

www.susanschadtpress.com

Published in 2022 by Susan Schadt Press, L.L.C.
New Orleans

Design by Tony Steck, DOXA/VANTAGE

Library of Congress Control Number: 2022904419

ISBN: 979-8-9850713-2-0

Printed by Friesen's in Altona, Canada